ASIA BOND MONITOR
MARCH 2024

ADB

ASIAN DEVELOPMENT BANK

ISBN 978-92-9270-640-1 (print); 978-92-9270-641-8 (PDF); 978-92-9270-642-5 (ebook)
ISSN 2219-1518 (print), 2219-1526 (PDF)
Publication Stock No. SGP240105-2
DOI: http://dx.doi.org/10.22617/SGP240105-2

Note:
ADB recognizes "China" as the People's Republic of China; "Hong Kong" as Hong Kong, China; "Korea" as the Republic of Korea; and "Vietnam" as Viet Nam.

Cover design by Erickson Mercado.

Contents

Emerging East Asian Local Currency Bond Markets: A Regional Update

Emerging East Asian Local Currency Bond Markets: A Regional Update

Executive Summary

Recent Developments in Financial Conditions in Emerging East Asia

Financial conditions marginally improved in emerging East Asia between 1 December 2023 and 29 February 2024.[1] Improvements in regional financial market conditions were largely supported by (i) expectations that the United States (US) Federal Reserve would ease its monetary policy later this year, (ii) moderating inflation, and (iii) robust economic performance in most regional economies. However, the recovery of financial conditions in the region was tempered by heightened uncertainties about the timing and magnitude of US monetary policy easing, given the continued strength of the US economy and the slowing pace of disinflation there. In addition, the People's Republic of China (PRC) weighed on the region's overall financial conditions during the review period due to heightened concerns over its economic slowdown, persistent deflation, and amplified trade tensions.

During the review period, most regional markets recorded equity gains, lowered risk premiums, and positive net foreign portfolios inflows, despite the marginal depreciation of regional currencies against a strong US dollar. Furthermore, equity markets gained in six out of nine of the region's economies, credit default swap spreads marginally fell by a regional (simple) average of 0.8 basis points if the PRC is excluded, and emerging East Asia's net foreign equity inflows totaled USD17.4 billion. The region's financial conditions were buoyed by robust economic growth, the expected ending of monetary tightening, and continued disinflation trends. At the same time, the increased likelihood of a delay in monetary easing and a strong US economic performance supported the US dollar, leading to a gross-domestic-product-weighted average depreciation of 1.0% for regional currencies versus the dollar. Most regional short-term bond yields also declined during the review period, but long-term bond yields rose slightly, tracking movements in advanced economies.

Risks to regional financial conditions remain tilted to the downside, largely due to uncertainties over the timing of US monetary policy easing. Possible disruptions to disinflationary momentum and spillover effects from the economic slowdown and deflation in the PRC could heighten the risk outlook.

Recent Developments in Local Currency Bond Markets in Emerging East Asia

At the end of December 2023, the local currency (LCY) bond market in emerging East Asia reached a size of USD25.2 trillion, expanding 2.5% quarter-on-quarter (q-o-q) in the fourth quarter (Q4) of 2023. Outstanding government bonds rose 3.9% q-o-q in Q4 2023, despite reduced issuance, due to a low volume of maturities in most regional markets. Government bonds accounted for 61.2% of total LCY bonds outstanding at the end of December. Meanwhile, the region's corporate bonds outstanding expanded marginally by 0.2% q-o-q in Q4 2023 as elevated interest rates and concerns about the property sector suppressed issuance in some markets. Aggregate LCY bonds outstanding among members of the Association of Southeast Asian Nations (ASEAN) totaled USD2.2 trillion, comprising 8.7% of the emerging East Asian market.

In Q4 2023, LCY bond issuance in emerging East Asia contracted 4.8% q-o-q to USD2.5 trillion as both government and corporate bond issuance declined. Government bond issuance fell 6.3% q-o-q to USD1.1 trillion as most regional governments had already fulfilled their borrowing requirements during the first 3 quarters of the year. LCY corporate bond issuance in Q4 2023 declined 7.8% q-o-q to USD0.9 trillion, dragged down by a contraction in corporate bond issuance in the PRC amid a weakened economic outlook and concerns over the property sector. ASEAN markets' combined LCY bond issuance totaled USD0.5 trillion in Q4 2023,

---

[1] Emerging East Asia is defined to include member states of the Association of Southeast Asian Nations (ASEAN) plus the People's Republic of China; Hong Kong, China; and the Republic of Korea.

equivalent to 21.2% of total emerging East Asian LCY bond issuance during the quarter.

Treasury bonds outstanding in emerging East Asia, as well as new issuances in Q4 2023, have generally been concentrated in longer-term maturities. Around 52.0% of Treasury bonds outstanding at the end of December had tenors of over 5 years. The corresponding share for Treasury bonds issued in Q4 2023 was 53.2%. At the end of 2023, the size-weighted average tenor of outstanding Treasury bonds was 8.9 years in emerging East Asia, with ASEAN markets' average being slightly higher at 9.0 years. The size-weighted average tenor of Treasury bond issuance in Q4 2023 was 7.4 years and 9.3 years in the markets of emerging East Asia and ASEAN, respectively.

Emerging East Asian LCY Treasury bonds are held primarily by relatively inactive traders such as domestic banks and insurance and pension funds. At the end of December, banks held an average of 36.7% of outstanding Treasury bonds in emerging East Asian markets, while insurance and pension funds held an average of 28.5%. Indonesia and the Republic of Korea have the most diversified investor profiles among all regional markets.

The ASEAN+3 sustainable bond market posted a robust expansion in 2023.[2] At the end of December, the outstanding amount of sustainable bonds in ASEAN+3 reached USD798.7 billion, buttressed by annual issuance totaling USD242.2 billion. The ASEAN+3 sustainable bond market expanded 29.3% year-on-year in 2023, which was much faster than the growth rates of the global (21.0%) and euro area (21.0%) sustainable bond markets. As a result, ASEAN+3's share of global sustainable bonds outstanding inched up to 20.1% in 2023 from 18.8% in 2022. Despite its rapid expansion, ASEAN+3's regional sustainable bond market only comprised 2.1% of its general bond market, which was much smaller than the euro area's corresponding 6.9% share.

Sustainable bond issuance in ASEAN markets in 2023 comprised a relatively higher share of LCY and long-term financing due to the greater participation of the public sector in the market. In ASEAN, the share of LCY financing in sustainable bond issuance was 80.6%, close to the LCY financing share in ASEAN general bond markets (82.3%). However, for ASEAN+3, the LCY financing share of sustainable bond issuance (73.4%) was lower than the corresponding share of general bond issuance (96.4%). Meanwhile, in ASEAN markets, around 84.5% of sustainable bond issuance in 2023 carried a tenor of over 5 years, which was higher than the corresponding share of 43.1% in ASEAN+3. The size-weighted average tenor for ASEAN sustainable bond issuance in 2023 was 14.7 years, compared with 6.2 years for ASEAN+3, largely driven by a higher share of public sector issuance in ASEAN markets.

AsianBondsOnline 2023 Bond Market Liquidity Survey

An overall improvement in liquidity conditions was noted in most emerging East Asian LCY bond market in 2023 compared with 2022, per the *AsianBondsOnline* annual bond market liquidity survey. Around two-thirds of respondents in the survey noted an improvement in liquidity amid relatively improved financial conditions, especially in the second half of the year, as the Federal Reserve signaled the end of its rate-hiking cycle. Most regional markets recorded a narrowing of bid–ask spreads and an increase in transaction sizes for both government and corporate bonds. Survey participants cited monetary policy and market sentiment as the most important domestic factors affecting liquidity in the market, while US monetary policy was the most important global factor. The 2023 survey also noted strong investor interest in sustainable bonds, with around three-fourths of participants indicating that they or their firms now trade and invest in sustainable bonds. The lack of hedging instruments in the region's bond markets remained a key structural issue in 2023 that needs further policy action.

---

[2] ASEAN+3 is defined to include member states of the Association of Southeast Asian Nations (ASEAN) plus the People's Republic of China; Hong Kong, China; Japan; and the Republic of Korea.

Developments in Regional Financial Conditions

Financial conditions in emerging East Asia marginally improved between 1 December 2023 and 29 February 2024 despite some weakening in January.[1] Financial market conditions were largely influenced by shifting expectations over the path of United States (US) monetary policy, moderating inflation, and improved economic performance across the region. In most regional markets during the review period, equity indexes gained, risk premiums narrowed, and positive net foreign portfolio equity and bond market inflows were recorded—all despite the marginal depreciation of regional currencies against the US dollar due to an expected delay in US rate cuts. Short-term bond yields declined for most markets in emerging East Asia over the expected end of monetary tightening, but long-term bond yields slightly rose in most markets, tracking bond yields in major advanced economies. Nevertheless, risks to regional financial conditions remained tilted to the downside, particularly regarding the uncertainty about the timing of US monetary easing, possible disruptions

to disinflationary momentum, as well as spillover effects from the economic slowdown and persistent deflation in the People's Republic of China (PRC).

In major advanced economies, both 2-year and 10-year local currency government bond yields slightly rose between 1 December 2023 and 29 February 2024 because of uncertainty about the timing of monetary policy adjustments (**Table A**). While financial markets largely expect advanced economy central banks to eventually ease their monetary stances, the recent release of economic data, particularly in the US, heightened uncertainties regarding the timing of their policy rate cuts.

In the US, 2-year and 10-year sovereign bond yields marginally edged up during the review period. Bond yields initially declined in December on expectations that the Federal Reserve would cut the federal funds target rate as early as March 2024. However, in January and February, US yields trended upward over rising uncertainty on

Table A: Changes in Financial Conditions in Major Advanced Economies and Select Emerging East Asian Markets from 1 December 2023 to 29 February 2024

	2-Year Government Bond Yield (bps)	10-Year Government Bond Yield (bps)	5-Year Credit Default Swap Spread (bps)	Equity Index (%)	FX Rate (%)
Major Advanced Economies					
Euro Area	22	5	–	10.4	(0.7)
Japan	13	1	(5)	13.6	(2.1)
United States	8	5	–	10.9	–
Select Emerging East Asian Markets					
China, People's Republic of	(37)	(33)	7	(0.5)	(0.8)
Hong Kong, China	(26)	3	–	(1.9)	(0.2)
Indonesia	(34)	(10)	(4)	3.6	(1.5)
Korea, Republic of	(14)	(22)	5	5.5	(1.9)
Malaysia	0	4	(0.5)	6.5	(1.5)
Philippines	13	1	(4)	11.2	(1.4)
Singapore	0.2	11	–	1.7	(0.9)
Thailand	(31)	(40)	(0.3)	(0.7)	(2.3)
Viet Nam	(39)	3	(0.9)	13.7	(1.5)

( ) = negative, – = not available, bps = basis points, FX = foreign exchange.

Note: A positive (negative) value for the FX rate indicates the appreciation (depreciation) of the local currency against the United States dollar.

Source: *AsianBondsOnline* calculations based on Bloomberg LP data.

---

[1] Emerging East Asia is defined to include member states of the Association of Southeast Asian Nations (ASEAN) plus the People's Republic of China; Hong Kong, China; and the Republic of Korea.

the timing of rate cuts following the hawkish comments of several Federal Reserve officials and stronger-than-expected economic data. In its 12–13 December 2023 Federal Open Market Committee (FOMC) meeting, the Federal Reserve left its policy rate unchanged at a range of 5.25%–5.50%, but the updated dot plot raised expectations for more rate cuts in 2024—with a total increase of 75 basis points (bps), up from 50 bps in the September projections. Financial markets also anticipated that the first rate cut would happen at the March 2024 FOMC meeting. As shown in the CME FedWatch Tool (**Figure A**), the likelihood of a 25 bps rate cut at the March FOMC meeting increased from 39.7% on 12 December to 65.4% on 13 December.

Several Federal Reserve officials, however, expressed caution in January and February about cutting interest rates in the near term, citing inflation concerns. For instance, Federal Reserve Bank of Cleveland President Loretta Mester said on 11 January that March was too soon for a rate cut, while Federal Reserve Governor Christopher J. Waller on 16 January echoed the sentiment that there was no reason to move quickly and the pace and size of rate cuts would depend on incoming data. During the 31 January FOMC press conference, Federal Reserve Chairman Jerome Powell said that a rate cut in March was unlikely. Federal Reserve officials confirmed these views with a hawkish tone in the minutes

of the January FOMC meeting, which were released in early February. The January meeting minutes noted that inflation had receded but remained above target and it would not be appropriate to adjust the policy rate until there was more confidence that inflation was trending down. This was reaffirmed by Federal Reserve Governor Michelle W. Bowman on 2 February, who cited that inflation needed to continue moving stably toward the 2.0% goal before the policy rate could be gradually lowered. On 14 February, Federal Reserve Vice Chair Michael Barr said that the soft-landing scenario was not certain yet. Federal Reserve Bank of Atlanta President Raphael Bostic also claimed on 15 February that he was not ready to support a rate cut due to ongoing risks. On 29 February, Federal Reserve Bank of New York President John Williams said he expects the Federal Reserve to cut rates later in the year. Consequently, market expectations on the probability of a rate cut in the March FOMC meeting dropped sharply from 70.2% on 11 January to 3.0% on 29 February (Figure A). Likewise, the probability that rates would also be left unchanged at the May FOMC meeting rose to 77.9% on 29 February from 2.3% on 11 January. This signaled a higher-for-longer rate and that the Federal Reserve could cut rates in the second half of the year. The CME FedWatch Tool on 29 February supported this assessment, reflecting a 53.9% likelihood of a 25 bps rate cut at the June FOMC meeting. Thus, the pace of Federal Reserve rate cuts remains uncertain.

US economic performance improved in the fourth quarter (Q4) of 2023 and early 2024. Gross domestic product (GDP) was expected to have expanded at an annualized 3.2% in Q4 2023, based on estimates that showed a continuation of the third quarter's annualized growth of 4.9%. Nonfarm payroll additions were reported at 275,000 in February, up from the previous month's 229,000. Meanwhile, the unemployment rate slightly increased to 3.9% in February from 3.7% in January. Consumer price inflation in January eased to 3.1% year-on-year (y-o-y) from December's 3.4% y-o-y, and producer price inflation also slowed to 0.9% y-o-y in January from 1.0% y-o-y in December. Based on the Federal Reserve's updated economic forecast released in December, 2024 GDP was downgraded slightly to 1.4% from 1.5%, and 2025 GDP was left unchanged at 1.8%. The Personal Consumption Expenditure inflation forecasts for 2024 and 2025 were revised downward to 2.4% y-o-y and 2.1% y-o-y, respectively, from 2.5% y-o-y and 2.2% y-o-y.

Figure A: Probability of a 25 bps Rate Cut at the Federal Open Market Committee Meeting on 19–20 March 2024

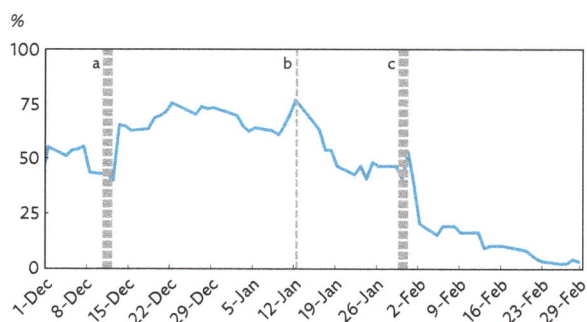

bps = basis points, FOMC = Federal Open Market Committee.
Note: Data are as of 29 February 2024.
a   FOMC December meeting with the Federal Reserve hinting of rate cuts in 2024.
b   Federal Reserve Bank of Cleveland President Loretta Mester says March is probably too early for a rate cut.
c   Federal Reserve Chairman Jerome Powell says rate cut unlikely in the March FOMC meeting.
Source: CME FedWatch Tool.

In the euro area, yields rose during the review period due to uncertainties regarding the European Central Bank's (ECB) monetary policy stance. While the ECB kept rates unchanged at its 14 December meeting, it announced the gradual reduction of its balance sheet by EUR7.5 billion per month on average, starting in the second half of 2024. During the 25 January ECB meeting, at which monetary policy was left unchanged, ECB President Christine Lagarde said that it was premature to discuss rate cuts and the central bank would continue to be data dependent. However, comments from some ECB officials suggested that a rate cut was forthcoming but the timing remained uncertain. ECB Governing Council Member Peter Kazimir said on 29 January that a rate cut would eventually occur, noting that a June rate cut was more likely than a rate cut in March. Likewise, on 9 February, Banco de España Governor Pablo Hernandez de Cos mentioned that the next ECB move was likely a rate cut. Minutes of the 25 January ECB meeting acknowledged that it was premature to discuss cutting rates but noted that inflation appeared to be on track to reach the ECB's target, possibly even faster than expected.

Inflation in the euro area continued to decline, while economic performance remained subdued. GDP in the euro area grew 0.1% y-o-y in Q4 2023, compared with 0.0% growth in the previous quarter. Consumer price inflation slightly eased to 2.6% y-o-y in February from 2.8% y-o-y in January. The ECB's December forecasts for 2024 consumer price inflation and GDP were downgraded to 2.7% y-o-y and 0.8% y-o-y, respectively, from 3.2% and 1.0% in September. On 7 March, the ECB left monetary policy unchanged but further lowered its 2024 inflation and GDP forecasts to 2.3% y-o-y and 0.6% y-o-y, respectively.

In Japan, bond yields rose slightly during the review period as the Bank of Japan (BOJ) signaled that it was gradually ending its easy monetary stance. At its 31 October meeting, the BOJ kept unchanged its –0.1% policy rate and scrapped the 1.0% ceiling on 10-year yields, saying that the 1.0% ceiling would be used as a reference. The BOJ has also been gradually reducing its Japan Government Bond purchases since the first quarter of 2023 (**Figure B**). While the policy rate was left unchanged at the 23 January meeting, BOJ Governor Kazuo Ueda said in a parliamentary meeting on 15 February that Japan's "virtuous cycle of wages and prices is strengthening." Japan's GDP performance also stabilized in Q4 2023, with a slower pace of decline at

Figure B: Bank of Japan's Purchases of Government Bonds

JPY trillion

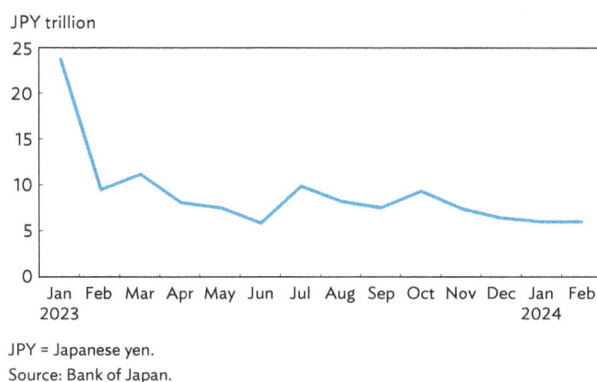

JPY = Japanese yen.
Source: Bank of Japan.

an annualized rate of –0.4% compared to –3.2% in the previous quarter. Consumer price inflation eased to 2.2% y-o-y in January from 2.6% y-o-y in December, approaching the central bank's 2.0% goal. In January, the BOJ's 2024 GDP forecast was upgraded slightly to 1.2% from 1.0% in October, and its 2024 inflation estimate was lowered to 2.4% y-o-y from 2.8% y-o-y in October. In the Summary of Opinions at the Monetary Policy Meeting released on 31 January, some members noted that, if the current trajectory of the economy is maintained, it may be appropriate to begin considering whether to "continue with its large-scale monetary easing measures, including the negative interest rate policy." However, uncertainties remain as BOJ Governor Kazuo Ueda, on 29 February, said that he could not yet say if the BOJ was close to achieving its inflation target.

Emerging East Asia's 2-year local currency government bond yields largely declined in most markets during the review period on the expected ending of monetary tightening, but 10-year bond yields trended up, tracking movements in advanced economies. Yields on 10-year government bonds declined in December over the likelihood that the Federal Reserve would begin rate-cutting in the first half of 2024. However, uncertainty about the Federal Reserve's expected monetary easing led to a rise in yields for most markets in January and February (**Figure C**).

Moderating inflation in the region helped keep yields from rising during the review period. Most economies recorded a decline in their respective inflation rates as supply shocks eased for some commodities (**Figure D**).

Figure C: Changes in 10-Year Local Currency Government Bond Yields in Select Emerging East Asian Markets

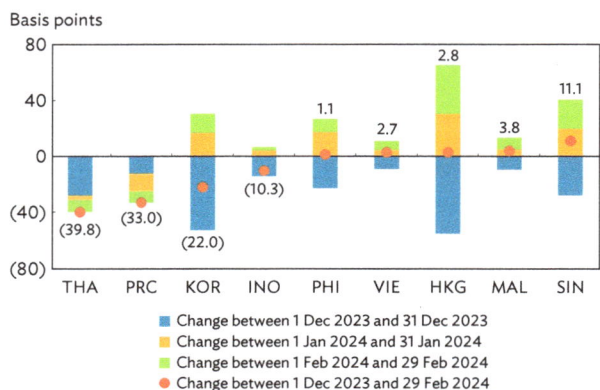

Basis points

( ) = negative; HKG = Hong Kong, China; INO = Indonesia; KOR = Republic of Korea; MAL = Malaysia; PHI = Philippines; PRC = People's Republic of China; SIN = Singapore; THA = Thailand; VIE = Viet Nam.

Note: The numbers above (below) each bar refer to the change between 1 December 2023 and 29 February 2024.

Source: *AsianBondsOnline* calculations based on Bloomberg LP data.

Moderating inflation combined with the Federal Reserve's expected easing have largely kept policy rates in the region unchanged, with some central banks hinting at a possible easing by the second half of the year (**Table B**). On 26 January, Bangko Sentral ng Pilipinas Governor Eli Remolona said that a rate cut was possible in 2024 but unlikely in the first half of the year. Similarly, on 21 February, Bank Indonesia Governor Perry Warjiyo noted that Bank Indonesia's outlook points to a rate cut sometime in the second half of the year. While the Bank of Thailand kept its monetary policy rate unchanged

on 7 February, two members voted in favor of a rate cut. On 8 February, Bank of Thailand Senior Director Sakkapop Panyanukul said that the central bank was ready to cut rates if consumption weakened. Moreover, central banks in the PRC and Viet Nam engaged in some form of easing last year to support their respective economies. In the PRC, the People's Bank of China announced a reduction in the reserve requirement ratio by 50 bps in January and reduced the 5-year loan prime rate by 25 bps to 3.95% in February. In Viet Nam, the State Bank of Vietnam lowered its refinancing rate to 4.50% via three cuts from April to June 2023.

Emerging East Asian currencies slightly weakened against the US dollar, largely driven by US monetary policy uncertainty (**Figure E**). Regional currencies weakened by a marginal 1.1% (simple average) and 1.0% (GDP-weighted average) from 1 December to 29 February. Collectively, regional currencies appreciated in December amid hints the Federal Reserve was approaching the end of its rate-hiking cycle. However, a majority of regional currencies weakened in January and February on a stronger US economy and hawkish tones from some Federal Reserve officials.

US monetary policy uncertainty marginally pushed up risk premiums in January. Risk premiums, as measured by credit default swap (CDS) spreads, fell marginally in the region during the review period by an average of 0.8 bps (simple) but widened by 0.1 bps (GDP-weighted), if excluding the PRC. CDS fell for most markets in December following expectations that the

Figure D: Inflation in Major Advanced Economies and Select Emerging East Asian Markets

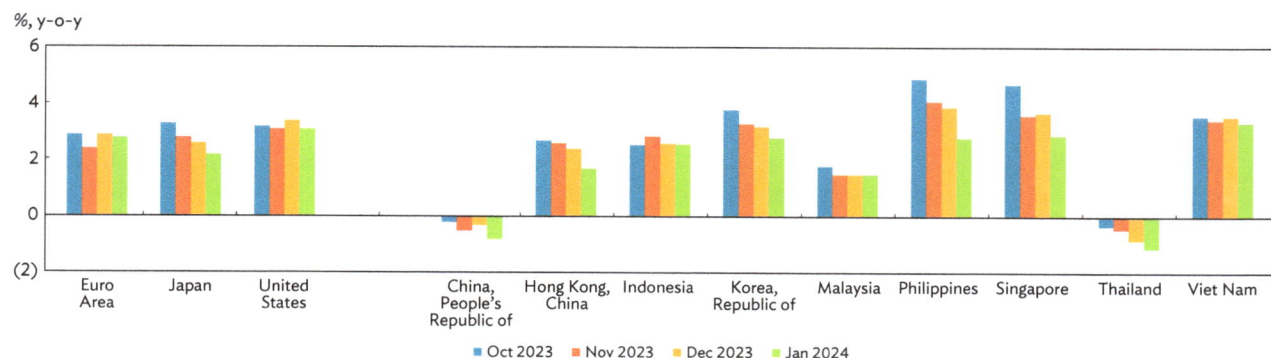

%, y-o-y

y-o-y = year-on-year.

Note: Data coverage is from October 2023 to January 2024.

Sources: Various local sources.

Table B: Changes in Monetary Stances in Major Advanced Economies and Select Emerging East Asian Markets

Economy	Policy Rate 1-Feb-2023 (%)	Rate Change (%)													Policy Rate 29-Feb-2024 (%)	Change in Policy Rates (basis points)
		Feb-2023	Mar-2023	Apr-2023	May-2023	Jun-2023	Jul-2023	Aug-2023	Sep-2023	Oct-2023	Nov-2023	Dec-2023	Jan-2024	Feb-2024		
Euro Area	2.00	↑0.50	↑0.50		↑0.25	↑0.25		↑0.25	↑0.25						4.00	↑ 200
Japan	(0.10)														(0.10)	♦ 0
United Kingdom	3.50	↑0.50	↑0.25		↑0.25	↑0.50		↑0.25							5.25	↑ 175
United States	4.75		↑0.25		↑0.25		↑0.25								5.50	↑ 75
China, People's Republic of	2.75					↓0.10		↓0.15							2.50	↓ 25
Indonesia	5.75									↑0.25					6.00	↑ 25
Korea, Republic of	3.50														3.50	♦ 0
Malaysia	2.75				↑0.25										3.00	↑ 25
Philippines	5.50	↑0.50	↑0.25								↑0.25				6.50	↑ 100
Singapore	–														–	–
Thailand	1.50		↑0.25		↑0.25			↑0.25	↑0.25						2.50	↑ 100
Viet Nam	6.00		↓0.50	↓0.50		↓0.50									4.50	↓ 150

( ) = negative, ♦ = no change, – = no data.

Notes:
1. Data coverage is from 1 February 2023 to 29 February 2024.
2. For the People's Republic of China, data used in the chart are for the 1-year medium-term lending facility rate. While the 1-year benchmark lending rate is the official policy rate of the People's Bank of China, market players use the 1-year medium-term lending facility rate as a guide for the monetary policy direction of the People's Bank of China.
3. The up (down) arrow for Singapore signifies monetary policy tightening (loosening) by its central bank. The Monetary Authority of Singapore utilizes the Singapore dollar nominal effective exchange rate to guide its monetary policy.

Sources: Various central bank websites.

Figure E: Changes in Select Emerging East Asian Currencies versus the United States Dollar

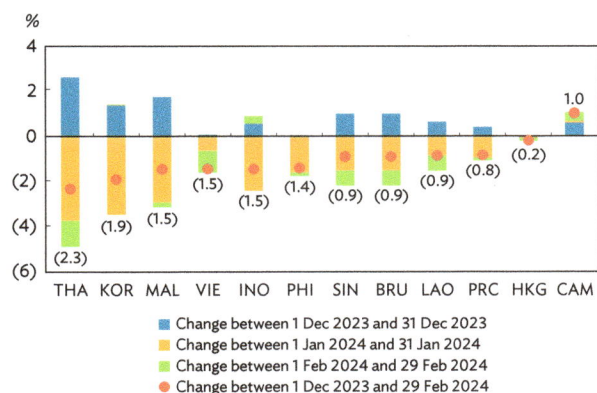

%

Legend:
- Change between 1 Dec 2023 and 31 Dec 2023
- Change between 1 Jan 2024 and 31 Jan 2024
- Change between 1 Feb 2024 and 29 Feb 2024
- Change between 1 Dec 2023 and 29 Feb 2024

Values (change between 1 Dec 2023 and 29 Feb 2024): THA (2.3), KOR (1.9), MAL (1.5), VIE (1.5), INO (1.5), PHI (1.4), SIN (0.9), BRU (0.9), LAO (0.9), PRC (0.8), HKG (0.2), CAM 1.0

( ) = negative; BRU = Brunei Darussalam; CAM = Cambodia; HKG = Hong Kong, China; INO = Indonesia; KOR = Republic of Korea; LAO = Lao People's Democratic Republic; MAL = Malaysia; PHI = Philippines; PRC = People's Republic of China; SIN = Singapore; THA = Thailand; VIE = Viet Nam.

Notes:
1. A positive (negative) value for the foreign exchange rate indicates the appreciation (depreciation) of the local currency against the United States dollar.
2. The numbers above (below) each bar refer to the change between 1 December 2023 and 29 February 2024.

Source: *AsianBondsOnline* calculations based on Bloomberg LP data.

Figure F: Changes in Credit Default Swap Spreads in Select Emerging East Asian Markets (senior 5-year)

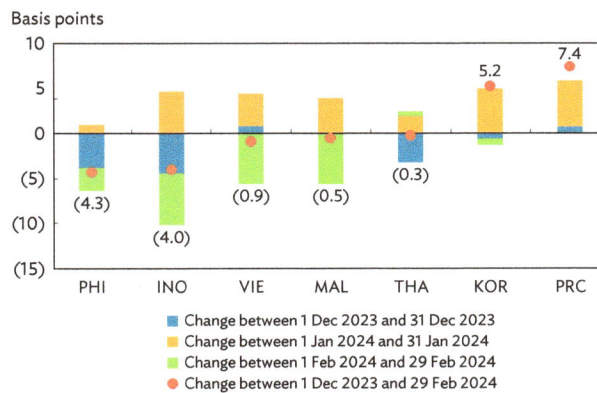

Basis points

Legend:
- Change between 1 Dec 2023 and 31 Dec 2023
- Change between 1 Jan 2024 and 31 Jan 2024
- Change between 1 Feb 2024 and 29 Feb 2024
- Change between 1 Dec 2023 and 29 Feb 2024

Values (change between 1 Dec 2023 and 29 Feb 2024): PHI (4.3), INO (4.0), VIE (0.9), MAL (0.5), THA (0.3), KOR 5.2, PRC 7.4

( ) = negative; INO = Indonesia; KOR = Republic of Korea; MAL = Malaysia; PHI = Philippines; PRC = People's Republic of China; THA = Thailand; VIE = Viet Nam.

Note: The numbers above (below) each bar refer to the change in spreads between 1 December 2023 and 29 February 2024.

Source: *AsianBondsOnline* calculations based on Bloomberg LP data.

Federal Reserve would begin cutting rates in 2024 (**Figure F**). However, heightened uncertainties over the timing of Federal Reserve rate cuts led to a rise in CDS spreads in all markets in January. CDS spreads recovered in most markets in February as market sentiment improved over the PRC's stimulus and fiscal measures to boost economic expansion. These measures included, among others, a reduction in the 5-year loan prime rate, a cut in the reserve requirement ratio, increased fiscal spending, frontloaded sovereign bond issuance, and low-interest loans to policy banks through the pledged supplementary facility. CDS spreads narrowed the most in the Philippines on improved sentiments as it posted the fastest growth in 2023 among all regional economies.

Regional equity markets were supported by robust economic performance in most markets. During the review period, regional equity markets gained an average of 5.9% (simple) and 4.7% (market-weighted) if the PRC and Hong Kong, China are excluded (**Figure G**). The gains were partly driven by better Q4 2023 GDP growth for most markets in the region versus the prior quarter (**Table C**). The growth outlook for most regional markets is also expected to improve in 2024 per the December 2023 *Asian Development Outlook*. In addition, equity markets were also supported by positive investor sentiment in December over the Federal Reserve's expected easing. On the other hand, equity markets in

Table C: Gross Domestic Product Growth in Select Emerging East Asian Markets (%, y-o-y)

Market	2023			2024ᵃ
	Q3	Q4	Full Year	
China, People's Republic of	4.90	5.20	5.20	4.50
Hong Kong, China	4.10	4.30	3.20	3.30
Indonesia	4.94	5.04	5.05	5.00
Korea, Republic of	1.40	2.20	1.40	2.20
Malaysia	3.30	3.00	3.70	4.60
Philippines	6.00	5.60	5.60	6.20
Singapore	1.00	2.20	1.10	2.50
Thailand	1.40	1.70	1.90	3.30
Viet Nam	5.33	6.72	5.05	6.00

Q3 = third quarter, Q4 = fourth quarter, y-o-y = year-on-year.
ᵃ Forecasts for 2024 are based on the *Asian Development Outlook* December 2023.
Sources: Various local sources.

both the PRC and Hong Kong, China recorded losses amid weakening economic conditions and concerns over the property sector. In February, regional equity markets recovered following the Government of the PRC's stimulus measures and a slew of additional stock market support. For example, the China Securities Regulatory Commission initiated measures to support the stock market by encouraging institutional investors to increase investments, asking companies to increase stock buy-backs, and creating a task force to monitor short-selling. The China Securities Regulatory Commission also banned select institutional investors from selling stocks at the start and end of each of each trading day. In addition, government-owned financial institutions, such as Central Huijin Investment, have become more active in the A share market. The Shanghai and Shenzhen stock exchanges announced that they would step-up the monitoring of quantitative hedge funds. The Ministry of Housing and Urban–Rural Development also asked banks to fund a white list of key housing projects.

Emerging East Asian capital markets recorded net portfolio inflows of USD17.4 billion during the review period on expectations of US monetary easing (**Figure H**). The largest portfolio inflows were recorded in February at USD15.3 billion over improving economic performance in the region and the PRC's government stimulus measures to support the economy, boosting foreign investor sentiment. Meanwhile, bond inflows into regional bond markets totaled USD12.2 billion in December, following signals the Federal Reserve would ease its monetary stance (**Figure I**). By January, inflows narrowed to

Figure G: Changes in Equity Indexes in Select Emerging East Asian Markets

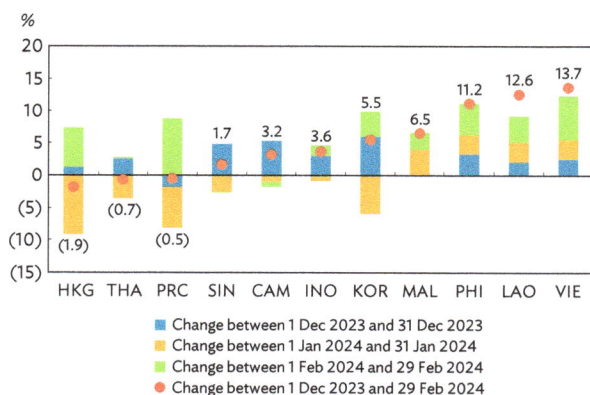

( ) = negative; CAM = Cambodia; HKG = Hong Kong, China; INO = Indonesia; KOR = Republic of Korea; LAO = Lao People's Democratic Republic; MAL = Malaysia; PHI = Philippines; PRC = People's Republic of China; SIN = Singapore; THA = Thailand; VIE = Viet Nam.
Note: The numbers above (below) each bar refer to the change between 1 December 2023 and 29 February 2024.
Source: *AsianBondsOnline* calculations based on Bloomberg LP data.

Figure H: Foreign Capital Flows in Select Emerging East Asian Equity Markets

USD billion

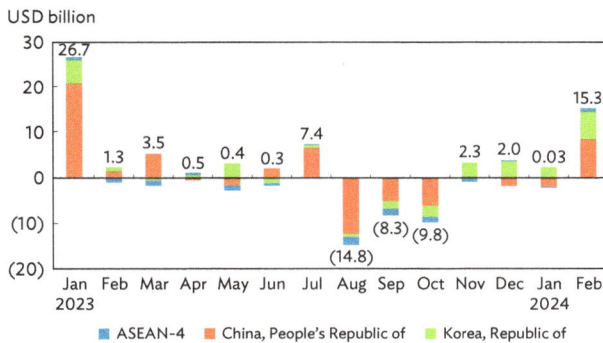

( ) = negative, USD = United States dollar.

Notes:
1. Data coverage is from 1 January 2023 to 29 February 2024.
2. The numbers above (below) each bar refer to net inflows (net outflows) for each month.
3. Emerging East Asia is defined to include member states of the Association of Southeast Asian Nations (ASEAN) plus the People's Republic of China; Hong Kong, China; and the Republic of Korea.
4. ASEAN-4 includes Indonesia, the Philippines, Thailand, and Viet Nam.

Source: Institute of International Finance.

Figure I: Foreign Capital Flows in Select Emerging East Asian Local Currency Bond Markets

USD billion

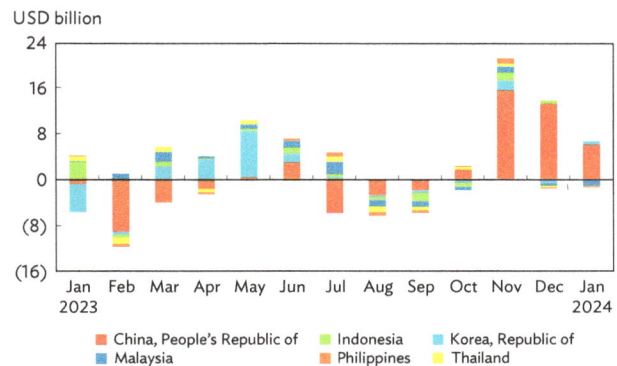

( ) = negative, USD = United States dollar.

Notes:
1. The Republic of Korea and Thailand provided data on bond flows. For the People's Republic of China, Indonesia, Malaysia, and the Philippines, month-on-month changes in foreign holdings of local currency government bonds were used as a proxy for bond flows.
2. Data are as of 31 January 2024.
3. Figures were computed based on 31 January 2024 exchange rates and do not include currency effects.

Sources: People's Republic of China (Bloomberg LP); Indonesia (Directorate General of Budget Financing and Risk Management, Ministry of Finance); Republic of Korea (Financial Supervisory Service); Malaysia (Bank Negara Malaysia); Philippines (Bureau of the Treasury); and Thailand (Thai Bond Market Association).

USD5.3 billion on uncertainty over the timing of US monetary policy easing.

The risk outlook for regional financial conditions is tilted to the downside, including not only uncertainty about the timing and magnitude of the Federal Reserve's monetary easing but also possible disruptions to disinflationary momentum and spillover effects from the economic slowdown and deflation in the PRC. The adverse effects of weather conditions and the intensification of geopolitical tensions around the world could further disrupt supply chains and reverse the process of disinflation in the region. Some geopolitical risks, such as Houthi attacks on ships in the Red Sea and a drought in the Panama Canal area, have caused a surge in container freight rates in Asia since late 2023.[2] Inflation persistence—due to factors such as adverse weather and other supply shocks—could still heighten

risk aversion among investors and consumers in the region, negatively affecting investment. In addition, weather-related disruptions have highlighted the need for additional investment in reducing carbon emissions. However, the region's large climate investment gap and its financing remain a challenge. **Box 1** discusses how blended finance helps close climate investment gaps by scaling up contributions of private capital. In the medium to long term, climate-related risks threaten development and economic growth. Financial markets are witnessing a growing interest in net zero investing as part of efforts to mitigate climate change, which also contributes to closing the climate finance gap. **Box 2** discusses the concept of net zero investing in greater detail.

---

[2] United Nations Conference on Trade and Development. 2024. "Navigating Troubled Waters Impact to Global Trade of Disruption of Shipping Routes in the Red Sea, Black Sea and Panama Canal." Geneva.

Box 1: The Growing Role of Blended Finance in Supporting Asia's Clean Energy Investments

Blended finance is an international public–private funding mechanism aimed at mobilizing private funds for infrastructure investment in emerging and developing economies (EMDEs). Given the growing need to decarbonize Asia's economy, expanding the scale of blended finance in clean energy requires innovative efforts by the international community to reform traditional development finance approaches.

Expanding Clean Energy Investment Requires Significant Financing

Asia faces substantial energy demand. The People's Republic of China (PRC), India, and Southeast Asia together will account for an estimated 70% of the world's growth in electricity demand during 2023-2025 (International Energy Agency [IEA] 2023).

To achieve net zero greenhouse gas (GHG) emissions, Asia needs to increase its annual clean energy annual investments from USD623 billion in 2022 to USD1,386 billion during 2026–2030 and USD1,658 billion during 2031–2035 (IEA 2023). **Table B1.1** shows that the PRC accounted for approximately 80% of total clean energy investment in Asia in 2022. As other Asian economies increase their clean energy investments over time, the PRC's share of the regional total is expected to drop to 62% during 2026–2030 and 57% during 2031–2035. To both promote decarbonization and meet

growing electricity demand, other Asian economies will need to increase their investments by about 6–8 times over current levels by 2031–2035. Even excluding the PRC, Asia's clean energy investments (derived from adding Southeast Asia, India, and "Other Asia") will be the largest in the EMDEs.

EMDEs, excluding the PRC, represent nearly 70% of the world's population, but their clean energy investment accounts for only 20% of the global total. This clearly reflects a shortage of private capital available for such investment due to political, economic, and exchange rate risks. Blended finance—which entails allocating more public funds initially and then gradually reducing this allocation as private capital increases—can be helpful for EMDEs with a track record of implementing such projects (Shirai 2023). Public funds can reduce risks borne by private investors through equity investments, loans, guarantees, grants, and technical assistance.

Blended Finance and Credit Ratings

One major constraint to scaling up private capital contributions for clean energy investments is the relatively low credit ratings of EMDEs. Many global investors have been subject to stringent financial regulations since the global financial crisis. They tend to prioritize investment-grade bonds with a credit rating of BBB or higher, and thus invest mainly in developed and some large emerging

Table B1.1: Annual Clean Investment Required under the Net Zero Scenario (USD billion)

| | 2015 | 2022 | Net Zero Scenario | | |
			(1) 2026–2030	(2) 2031–2035	(2)/2020 Level
EMDEs	538	773	2,222	2,805	4
People's Republic of China	287	511	853	947	2
EMDEs excluding PRC	251	262	1,369	1,858	7
Southeast Asia	28	30	185	244	8
India and Other Asia	76	82	348	467	6
Africa	26	32	203	265	8
Latin America	63	66	243	332	5
Middle East and Eurasia	57	52	390	550	11
Asian EMDEs	391	623	1,386	1,658	3

EMDE = emerging and developing economy, PRC = People's Republic of China, USD = United States dollar.
Notes:
1. Regions are defined based on International Energy Agency (IEA) classifications.
2. The sum of regional data does not add up to total amount due to rounding.
Source: Author's calculations based on International Energy Agency (2023).

This box was written by Sayuri Shirai, PhD, an advisor for sustainable policies at the Asian Development Bank Institute, a professor at the Faculty of Policy Management of Keio University, and a former policy board member of the Bank of Japan. The content of this box is based on Shirai, Sayuri. 2023. Asia's Clean Energy Investment Needs and the Role of Blended Finance. *Asia Pathways*. 10 August.

continued on next page

Box 1   *continued*

economies. However, since about 80% of EMDE government bonds have a speculative rating of BB or lower, with high political and exchange rate risks, private investors often hesitate to invest in these economies. Thus, financial institutions that invest in speculative-grade securities require additional capital to build up a buffer, and these investments often do not provide enough returns to make up for the additional capital costs.

The funding environment for EMDEs has deteriorated further since the United States (US) Federal Reserve began normalizing monetary policy in 2022 due to rising inflation. This has led to the depreciation of EMDE currencies against the US dollar and amplified domestic inflation in developing economies through higher imported inflation. Many central banks in these markets reacted to inflation and capital outflows by raising their policy rates. Furthermore, public debt levels in EMDEs were expanded to cope with the coronavirus disease (COVID-19) crisis, making it even more challenging to mobilize new funds from the private sector.

Figure B1 shows the sovereign bond ratings and per capita GHG emissions of markets in Asia. Emission-intensive markets with low credit ratings face challenges to attracting private capital and thus may need to rely more heavily on public funds. Blended finance may not be suitable for low-income economies with high degrees of debt stress. In such economies, debt-for-climate swaps and grants based on climate performance could be explored (Shirai 2023).

To achieve net-zero goals in low-income economies, a greater share of concessional funds will be needed to bolster the use

Figure B1: Per Capita Greenhouse Gas Emissions (metric tons, CO_2 equivalent) **and Sovereign Credit Ratings**

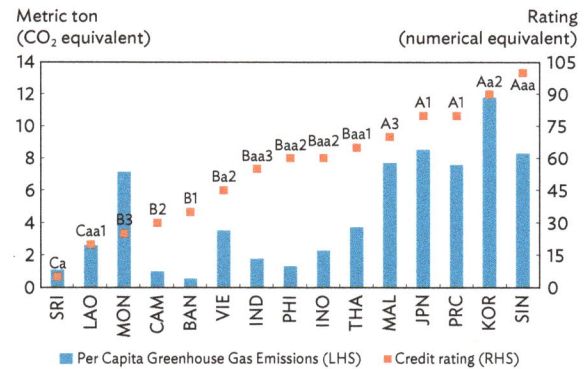

BAN = Bangladesh, CAM = Cambodia, CO_2 = carbon dioxide, IND = India, INO = Indonesia, JPN = Japan, KOR = Republic of Korea, LAO = Lao People's Democratic Republic, LHS = left-hand side, MAL = Malaysia, MON = Mongolia, PHI = Philippines, PRC = People's Republic of China, RHS = right-hand side, SIN = Singapore, SRI = Sri Lanka, THA = Thailand, VIE = Viet Nam.

Note: The sovereign credit rating is adjusted to the numerical number from 0 (CCC) to 100 (AAA).

Source: Author's illustration based on S&P Global and Our World in Data.

of blended finance. The IEA (2023) has estimated that such funds would need to account for about 10%–20% of total clean energy investments in Asia. In Africa, where investments are often perceived to carry higher risks compared to Asia, nearly half of clean energy blended finance would need to be concessional (**Table B1.2**).

Table B1.2: Annual Clean Investment and Concessional Finance Required under the Net Zero Scenario (USD billion)

			Net Zero Scenario					
	2015	2022	(a) 2026–2030	(b) Concessional Finance	(b)/(a) (%)	(a) 2031–2035	(b) Concessional Finance	(b)/(a) (%)
EMDEs excluding PRC	250	262	1,369	83	6	1,858	101	5
Southeast Asia	28	30	185	7	4	244	9	4
India and Other Asia	76	82	348	16	5	467	20	4
Africa	26	32	203	37	18	265	46	17
Latin America	63	66	243	13	5	332	14	4
Middle East and Eurasia	57	52	390	10	3	550	11	2

EMDEs = emerging and developing economies, PRC = People's Republic of China, USD = United States dollar.
Source: Author's calculations based on International Energy Agency (2023).

continued on next page

Box 1 *continued*

Just Energy Transition Partnerships and Their Challenges

Just Energy Transition Partnerships, which were announced at the United Nations Climate Change Conference in Glasgow in 2021, are a collective financial mechanism to help EMDEs achieve their GHG reduction targets by replacing coal-fired power plants with clean energy. Advanced economies and the Glasgow Financial Alliance for Net Zero have jointly pledged to mobilize climate funds for Just Energy Transition Partnerships. Such partnerships were concluded with South Africa (USD8.5 billion) in 2021, Indonesia (USD20.0 billion) and Viet Nam (USD15.5 billion) in 2022, and Senegal (USD2.7 billion) in 2023. The recipient economies are required to develop emission reduction plans, including a path toward reduced coal dependence and a smooth transition for impacted industries and workers.

Final Remarks

It may be important for advanced economies to consider taking more innovative actions to increase the use of blended finance. Bilateral overseas development assistance and other development finance could benefit from increased coordination on clean energy projects and in relevant sectors through the sharing of skills, knowledge, and funds, given that limited financial resources are available among donor economies due to challenging domestic economic and fiscal conditions. The existence of parallel initiatives by Group of 7 (G7) members in the same sectors heightens the risk of the inefficient channeling of limited funds. In some cases, a clearer division of labor among G7 members based on preferential geographies—for example, the European Union focusing on Africa, the US on Latin America, and Japan on Asia—might prove to be more efficient and impactful by reducing fragmentation problems. Further, advanced economies could reexamine their traditional development finance approaches and steer more funds to blended finance through guarantees and equity investments. In conclusion, it may be time for G7 economies to assume greater leadership in promoting carbon neutrality among EMDEs.

References

International Energy Agency. 2023. *Scaling up Private Finance for Clean Energy in Emerging and Developing Economies*. https://www.iea.org/reports/scaling-up-private-finance-for-clean-energy-in-emerging-and-developing-economies.

Sayuri Shirai. 2023. *Global Climate Change Challenges, Innovative Finance, and Green Central Banking*. Manila: Asian Development Bank. https://www.adb.org/publications/global-climate-challenges-innovative-finance-and-green-central-banking.

Box 2: Net Zero Investing

The transition to Net Zero to mitigate the impacts of global warming will continue to influence investor behavior. Therefore, investors should align their equity and corporate bond allocations in accordance with Net Zero principles. Investors must reassess traditional asset allocation practices to reflect the fundamental alteration to the global economy caused by climate change. To better understand the implications of the transition to Net Zero, we compared multiple asset allocation variations against a standard, non-climate aligned asset allocation comprising 60% equities and 40% fixed income.

Pursuing Net Zero Asset Allocations

Net Zero investing involves not only pursuing a low-carbon portfolio but also financing the process of transitioning to a green economy. Integrating Net Zero targets into asset allocations also provides benefits from a risk-return perspective. The rise of the low-carbon economy is presenting new possibilities to investors, as innovative business models are introduced and the global economy undergoes unprecedented structural transformation. The future is unknowable, however, current trends highlight the importance of immediately integrating Net Zero considerations into investments to be better positioned for the economic implications of a carbon-neutral world.

Targeting Net Zero asset allocations entails several sub-objectives that collectively contribute to acheving Net Zero emissions by 2050 (**Figure B2.1**).

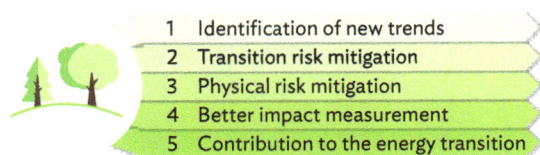

Figure B2.1: Primary Benefits of Net Zero Investing

1 Identification of new trends
2 Transition risk mitigation
3 Physical risk mitigation
4 Better impact measurement
5 Contribution to the energy transition

Source: Amundi.

Integrating Net Zero Targets into Portfolios

The two main building blocks for Net Zero portfolios are Net Zero Contribution portfolios and the Net Zero Transition portfolios. The former refers to investments in firms and projects that promote the green economy through the development of new technologies and innovative solutions. Net Zero Contributions generally increase the green share of an allocation by investing in climate-friendly endeavors. The latter, Net Zero Transition portfolios, seek a gradual decarbonization of investments in alignment with the Paris Agreement and in support of reaching global carbon neutrality by 2050. This can be achieved by managing equity or credit investments in favor of corporates that are contributing to limiting global warming to 1.5°C above pre-industrial levels and away from issuers that fail to demonstrate sufficient commitment to a low-carbon economy.

Divestment should be used as a last resort, and reducing the emissions linked to a portfolio should involve more than just shunning investments in high-polluting sectors. Institutional investors can use their influence to encourage companies to pursue a Net Zero transition and contribute to emissions reductions.

The Financial Impact of a Net Zero Portfolio

A comparison of Net Zero asset allocations with standard, non-climate aligned asset allocations reveals differences in financial performance and risk; sectoral composition; environmental, social, and governance (ESG) issues; and climate performance (i.e., ESG ratings and carbon emissions) (**Figure B2.2**).

Integrating Net Zero targets into asset allocations has a short-term impact on portfolio metrics, primarily in the form of more Tracking Errors (TEs). This is not surprising since the global economy has not yet fully adopted decarbonization. Further, while short-term financial costs are limited, these can be more than offset in the long term as corporates worldwide gradually transition to low-carbon models.

Net Zero asset allocations have outperformed standard asset allocations in ESG and climate metrics, while also contributing to reduced carbon intensity. At the sectoral level, Net Zero asset allocations deviate the most from standard allocations in the energy and technology sectors, suggesting that Net Zero investors will be better prepared to continue capitalizing on structural economic changes that are already underway.

This box was prepared by Monica Defend (head) of Amundi Investment Institute. The write-up is a revised and shortened summary based on Mortier, Vincent, and Jean-Jacques Barberis. 2023. "Net Zero Investing and Its Impact on a 60–40 Allocation." Amundi Investment Institute. 7 June.

continued on next page

Box 2 *continued*

Figure B2.2: Performance of Standard versus Paris-Aligned Benchmarks Passive Allocations (Linear and Annual)

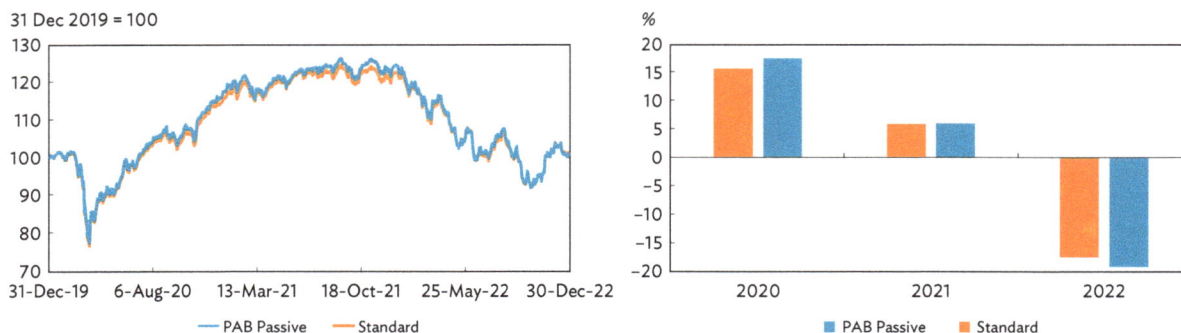

PAB = Paris-aligned benchmark.
Notes: The data are from 31 December 2019 to 30 December 2022. Past performance does not predict future returns.
Source: Amundi based on MSCI data.

Analysis by the Amundi Institute has identified three main aspects of Net Zero asset allocations (**Table B2**):

1. The short-term impact on key portfolio metrics is evidenced by higher TEs, especially for the Net Zero Active asset allocations with a contribution pocket, since the transition to a low-carbon economy is in the nascent stage. However, as Europe is further along in the energy transition process than developing economies, it offers hope as the TEs for European institutional investors pursuing Net Zero strategies are likely lower than in emerging markets.

2. Standard and Paris-aligned benchmark passive asset allocations have exhibited similar financial performances, with the latter slightly outperforming in 2020 and 2021.

3. There has been significant improvement in ESG and climate metrics in Net Zero asset allocations compared to standard ones. Active asset allocations have effected reductions in carbon intensity, while many corporates have set science-based targets.

Table B2: Composition of Different Asset Allocations (%)

			Standard Passive	PAB Passive	Net Zero Active	With Green Contribution[a]
Equity	60%	World	40	40	40	30
		EM	20	20	20	20
		Green	–	–	–	10
Fixed income	40%	US IG Corp.	20	20	20	15
		EU IG Corp.	20	20	20	15
		Green	–	–	–	10

EM = emerging market, EU = Europe, IG = investment grade, PAB = Paris-aligned benchmark, US = United States.
Notes:
1. Colors: blue = active, green = green investments, orange = passive.
2. Data are as of April 2023.
[a] Net Zero Active with Green Contribution AA, ex-ante analysis only.
Source: Amundi.

Bond Market Developments in the Fourth Quarter of 2023

Section 1. Local Currency Bonds Outstanding

At the end of December 2023, the local currency (LCY) bond market in emerging East Asia reached a size of USD25.2 trillion, expanding 9.2% year-on-year (y-o-y).[3] Annual growth in emerging East Asian LCY bonds outstanding outpaced that of the United States (US) (8.2% y-o-y) and the European Union (EU-20) (6.3% y-o-y). At the end of December, the size of emerging East Asian LCY bond market was equivalent to 66.7% of that of the US (USD37.8 trillion) and 117.3% of the EU-20 bond market (USD21.5 trillion) (**Figure 1**).

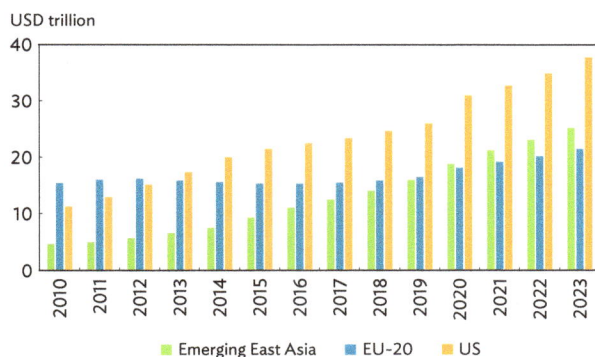

Figure 1: Local Currency Bonds Outstanding in Emerging East Asia, the EU-20, and the United States

USD trillion

(Bar chart with years 2010–2023 on the x-axis, showing Emerging East Asia, EU-20, and US)

■ Emerging East Asia ■ EU-20 ■ US

EU = European Union, US = United States, USD = United States dollar.

Notes:
1. Emerging East Asia is defined to include the Association of Southeast Asian Nations plus the People's Republic of China; Hong Kong, China; and the Republic of Korea.
2. The EU-20 includes the member markets of Austria, Belgium, Croatia, Cyprus, Estonia, Finland, France, Germany, Greece, Ireland, Italy, Latvia, Lithuania, Luxembourg, Malta, the Netherlands, Portugal, Slovakia, Slovenia, and Spain.

Sources: People's Republic of China (CEIC Data Company); Hong Kong, China (Hong Kong Monetary Authority); EU-20 (European Central Bank); Indonesia (Bank Indonesia; Directorate General of Budget Financing and Risk Management, Ministry of Finance; and Indonesia Stock Exchange); Republic of Korea (Bank of Korea and KG Zeroin Corporation); Malaysia (Bank Negara Malaysia); Philippines (Bureau of the Treasury and Bloomberg LP); Singapore (Monetary Authority of Singapore and Bloomberg LP); Thailand (Bank of Thailand); United States (Securities Industry and Financial Markets Association and Bloomberg LP); and Viet Nam (Vietnam Bond Market Association and Bloomberg LP).

Emerging East Asian LCY bonds outstanding expanded faster in the fourth quarter (Q4) of 2023 than in the previous quarter, driven by growth in government bonds. The regional LCY bond market expanded 2.5% quarter-on-quarter (q-o-q) in Q4 2023, with most markets posting positive quarterly growth (**Table 1**). Despite a contraction in issuance during the quarter, outstanding government bonds rose 3.9% q-o-q, compared with 3.0% q-o-q in the third quarter (Q3) of 2023, due to smaller volume of maturities in most regional markets, particularly the larger markets of the People's Republic of China (PRC) and the Republic of Korea. Meanwhile, growth in the region's corporate bond market slowed to 0.2% q-o-q in Q4 2023 from 1.5% q-o-q in the prior quarter amid higher interest rates and concerns about the property sector in some markets. Viet Nam and Thailand recorded contractions in LCY bonds outstanding due to a relatively large volume of maturities and weak issuance, respectively (**Figure 2**).

LCY bonds outstanding in Association of Southeast Asian Nation (ASEAN) markets totaled USD2.2 trillion at the end of December, comprising 8.7% of the emerging East Asian LCY bond market. The PRC's LCY bond market (USD20.1 trillion) represented 79.8% of the region's total at the end of December, while that of the Republic of Korea (USD2.5 trillion) accounted for 9.9% (**Figure 3**). Government bonds (USD15.4 trillion) comprised a majority of regional LCY bonds (61.2%), followed by corporate bonds (USD9.2 trillion) and central bank bonds (USD0.6 trillion) with shares of 36.5% and 2.2%, respectively.

Outstanding LCY Treasury bonds in emerging East Asian markets are generally concentrated in longer-term maturities (**Figure 4**). At the end of December, the size-weighted average tenor of Treasury bonds outstanding in the region was 8.9 years, slightly lower than ASEAN markets' average of 9.0 years. Overall, 52.0% of Treasury bonds outstanding in emerging East Asia had tenors of over 5 years. In ASEAN markets,

---

[3] Emerging East Asia is defined to include member states of the Association of Southeast Asian Nations (ASEAN) plus the People's Republic of China; Hong Kong, China; and the Republic of Korea.

Table 1: Size and Composition of Select Emerging East Asian Local Currency Bond Markets

	Q4 2022		Q3 2023		Q4 2023			Growth Rate (%) Q4 2023	
	Amount (USD billion)	% of GDP	Amount (USD billion)	% of GDP	Amount (USD billion)	% share	% of GDP	q-o-q	y-o-y
China, People's Republic of									
Total	18,879	108.1	19,031	111.4	20,098	100.0	113.1	2.7	9.6
Treasury and Other Government	11,870	68.0	12,194	71.3	13,096	65.2	73.7	4.5	13.5
Central Bank	2	0.01	2	0.01	2	0.01	0.01	0.0	0.0
Corporate	7,007	40.1	6,835	40.0	7,000	34.8	39.4	(0.4)	2.8
Hong Kong, China									
Total	355	98.6	385	103.0	387	100.0	101.1	0.3	9.1
Treasury and Other Government	31	8.5	37	9.9	36	9.4	9.5	(1.5)	19.3
Government	155	43.0	158	42.4	161	41.5	42.0	1.2	4.0
Corporate	170	47.1	190	50.7	190	49.1	49.6	(0.2)	12.0
Indonesia									
Total	382	30.4	399	29.8	411	100.0	30.3	2.7	6.4
Treasury and Other Government	350	27.8	366	27.3	377	91.7	27.8	2.6	6.5
Central Bank	3	0.3	4	0.3	4	1.0	0.3	10.7	19.3
Corporate	29	2.3	29	2.1	30	7.3	2.2	3.5	3.2
Korea, Republic of									
Total	2,346	150.8	2,347	159.6	2,497	100.0	161.2	1.6	8.4
Treasury and Other Government	907	58.3	893	60.7	933	37.4	60.2	(0.3)	4.7
Central Bank	89	5.7	93	6.3	94	3.8	6.1	(3.1)	8.0
Corporate	1,350	86.7	1,361	92.5	1,470	58.9	94.9	3.1	10.9
Malaysia									
Total	424	123.6	422	127.5	437	100.0	128.1	1.2	7.5
Treasury and Other Government	238	69.5	240	72.5	249	56.9	72.9	1.4	8.8
Central Bank	0.2	0.1	3	1.0	4	0.9	1.1	11.0	1,620.0
Corporate	185	54.0	179	54.1	184	42.2	54.1	0.8	3.9
Philippines									
Total	201	50.8	210	50.2	217	100.0	49.5	1.0	7.4
Treasury and Other Government	164	41.4	171	40.8	178	82.1	40.7	2.1	8.4
Central Bank	9	2.2	12	2.9	11	5.3	2.6	(6.2)	32.5
Corporate	29	7.3	27	6.6	27	12.6	6.2	(2.6)	(5.6)
Singapore									
Total	492	96.0	510	104.3	542	100.0	106.3	2.6	8.5
Treasury and Other Government	174	34.0	183	37.3	195	35.9	38.2	2.9	10.0
Central Bank	186	36.2	204	41.7	223	41.1	43.6	5.3	18.2
Corporate	132	25.8	123	25.2	125	23.0	24.5	(2.3)	(6.9)
Thailand									
Total	452	89.9	455	92.9	483	100.0	92.0	(0.5)	5.5
Treasury and Other Government	253	50.5	256	52.3	276	57.1	52.5	0.96	7.3
Central Bank	69	13.8	67	13.7	65	13.5	12.4	(8.9)	(7.2)
Corporate	129	25.6	132	26.9	142	29.4	27.0	1.1	8.7
Viet Nam									
Total	106	26.3	110	26.8	109	100.0	26.0	(0.4)	6.2
Treasury and Other Government	71	17.6	78	19.1	80	73.1	19.0	2.0	16.0
Central Bank	4	0.99	4	0.9	0	0.0	0.0	(100.0)	(100.0)
Corporate	31	7.7	28	6.7	29	26.9	7.0	6.8	(2.3)
Emerging East Asia									
Total	23,637	103.7	23,869	106.5	25,182	100.0	108.1	2.5	9.2
Treasury and Other Government	14,059	61.7	14,418	64.3	15,420	61.2	66.2	3.9	12.5
Central Bank	517	2.3	548	2.4	564	2.2	2.4	(0.02)	8.7
Corporate	9,061	39.8	8,904	39.7	9,197	36.5	39.5	0.2	4.1
Japan									
Total	10,164	238.1	9,034	231.0	9,670	100.0	230.4	1.1	2.3
Treasury and Other Government	9,382	219.8	8,339	213.2	8,918	92.2	212.5	0.98	2.2
Central Bank	34	0.8	13	0.3	27	0.3	0.6	96.9	(14.5)
Corporate	748	17.5	682	17.4	725	7.5	17.3	0.3	4.2

( ) = negative, GDP = gross domestic product, q-o-q = quarter-on-quarter, Q3 = third quarter, Q4 = fourth quarter, USD = United States dollar, y-o-y = year-on-year.

Notes:
1. For Singapore, corporate bonds outstanding are based on *AsianBondsOnline* estimates.
2. GDP data are from CEIC Data Company.
3. Bloomberg LP end-of-period local currency–USD rates are used.
4. Growth rates are calculated from a local currency base and do not include currency effects. For emerging East Asia, growth figures are based on 31 December 2023 currency exchange rates and do not include currency effects.

Sources: People's Republic of China (CEIC Data Company); Hong Kong, China (Hong Kong Monetary Authority); Indonesia (Bank Indonesia; Directorate General of Budget Financing and Risk Management, Ministry of Finance; and Indonesia Stock Exchange); Republic of Korea (Bank of Korea and KG Zeroin Corporation); Malaysia (Bank Negara Malaysia); Philippines (Bureau of the Treasury and Bloomberg LP); Singapore (Monetary Authority of Singapore and Bloomberg LP); Thailand (Bank of Thailand); and Viet Nam (Vietnam Bond Market Association and Bloomberg LP).

Figure 2: Growth of Select Emerging East Asian Local Currency Bond Markets in the Third and Fourth Quarters of 2023 (q-o-q, %)

( ) = negative; HKG = Hong Kong, China; INO = Indonesia; KOR = Republic of Korea; MAL = Malaysia; PHI = Philippines; PRC = People's Republic of China; Q3 = third quarter; Q4 = fourth quarter; q-o-q = quarter-on-quarter; SIN = Singapore; THA = Thailand; VIE = Viet Nam.

Notes:
1. For Singapore, corporate bonds outstanding are based on *AsianBondsOnline* estimates.
2. Growth rates are calculated from a local-currency base and do not include currency effects. For emerging East Asia, growth figures are based on 31 December 2023 currency exchange rates and do not include currency effects.

Sources: People's Republic of China (CEIC Data Company); Hong Kong, China (Hong Kong Monetary Authority); Indonesia (Bank Indonesia; Directorate General of Budget Financing and Risk Management, Ministry of Finance; and Indonesia Stock Exchange); Republic of Korea (Bank of Korea and KG Zeroin Corporation); Malaysia (Bank Negara Malaysia); Philippines (Bureau of the Treasury and Bloomberg LP); Singapore (Monetary Authority of Singapore and Bloomberg LP); Thailand (Bank of Thailand); and Viet Nam (Vietnam Bond Market Association and Bloomberg LP).

Figure 3: Local Currency Bonds Outstanding in Emerging East Asia by Economy and Type of Bond as of 31 December 2023

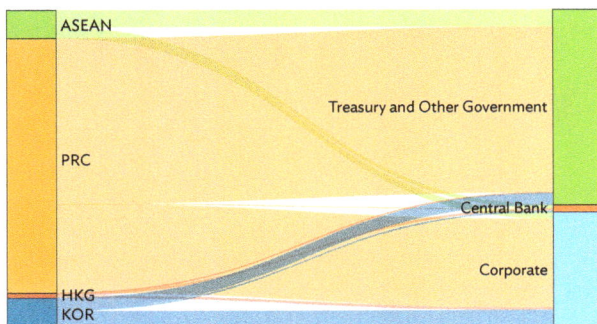

ASEAN = Association of Southeast Asian Nations; HKG = Hong Kong, China; KOR = Republic of Korea; PRC = People's Republic of China.

Note: ASEAN comprises the markets of Indonesia, Malaysia, the Philippines, Singapore, Thailand, and Viet Nam.

Source: *AsianBondsOnline* calculations based on various local sources.

Figure 4: Maturity Structure of Local Currency Treasury Bonds Outstanding in Select Emerging East Asian Markets as of 31 December 2023

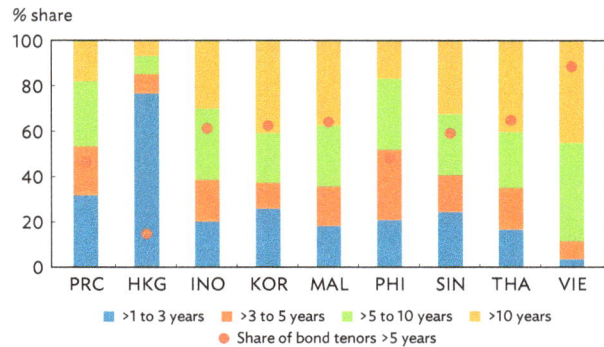

HKG = Hong Kong, China; INO = Indonesia; KOR = Republic of Korea; MAL = Malaysia; PHI = Philippines; PRC = People's Republic of China; SIN = Singapore; THA = Thailand; VIE = Viet Nam.

Note: Treasury bonds are local-currency-denominated, fixed-income securities with maturities longer than 1 year and issued by the government.

Sources: People's Republic of China (Bloomberg LP); Hong Kong, China (Hong Kong Monetary Authority); Indonesia (Directorate General of Budget Financing and Risk Management, Ministry of Finance); Republic of Korea (Bloomberg LP); Malaysia (Bank Negara Malaysia Fully Automated System for Issuing/Tendering); Philippines (Bureau of the Treasury); Singapore (Monetary Authority of Singapore); Thailand (Bank of Thailand); and Viet Nam (Bloomberg LP).

62.3% of Treasury bonds outstanding had maturities of over 5 years, with Viet Nam's market having the highest share at 88.5%. Meanwhile, Hong Kong, China had 14.8% of its outstanding Treasury bonds carrying maturities of over 5 years at the end of December.

The majority of emerging East Asian LCY Treasury bonds are held by relatively inactive traders such as domestic banks and insurance and pension funds (**Figure 5**). Scores on the Herfindahl–Hirschman Index, which measures investor concentration in a particular market, remained high in Viet Nam and the PRC. Among all emerging East Asian Treasury bond markets, banks accounted for the largest average holdings share at 36.7%, followed by insurance and pension funds at 28.5%. Bank holdings of Treasury bonds were the largest in the PRC (69.4%) and the Philippines (46.2%), while insurance and pension funds holdings were higher in Viet Nam (59.8%) and Thailand (44.5%). Indonesia has the region's most diversified investor profile, with banks, the largest holders of Treasury bonds in the domestic market, only accounting for 26.5% of the total. The Republic of Korea's Treasury bond market also has a relatively low Herfindahl–Hirschman Index score, reflecting a

Figure 5: Investor Profiles of Local Currency Treasury Bonds in Select Emerging East Asian Markets

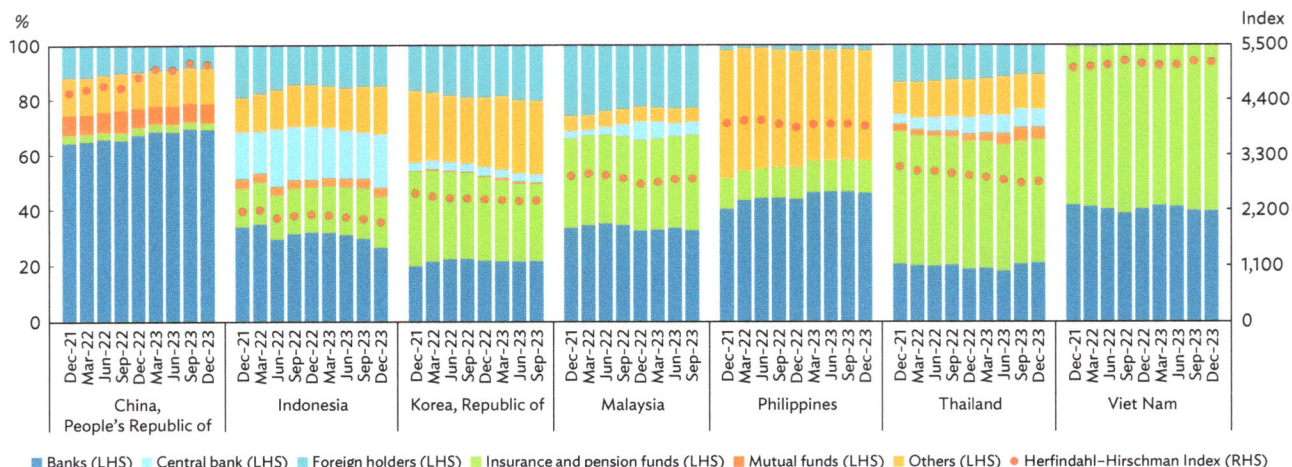

LHS = left-hand side, RHS = right-hand side.
Notes:
1. Data for the Republic of Korea and Malaysia are up to September 2023.
2. "Others" include government institutions, individuals, securities companies, custodians, private corporations, and all other investors not elsewhere classified.
3. The Herfindahl–Hirschman Index is a commonly accepted measure of market concentration. In this case, the index was used to measure the investor profile diversification of the local currency bond markets and is calculated by summing the squared share of each investor group in the bond market.
Sources: People's Republic of China (CEIC Data Company); Indonesia (Directorate General of Budget Financing and Risk Management, Ministry of Finance); Republic of Korea (Bank of Korea); Malaysia (Bank Negara Malaysia); Philippines (Bureau of the Treasury); Thailand (Bank of Thailand); and Viet Nam (Ministry of Finance).

diversified investor profile, with the largest investor group, insurance and pension funds, holding 27.8% of Treasury bonds outstanding. Insurance and pension funds were also the dominant investor group in the less-diversified markets of Malaysia (34.6%), Thailand (44.5%), and Viet Nam (59.8%).

Section 2. Local Currency Bond Issuance

Despite the q-o-q issuance contraction in Q4 2023, emerging East Asia's annual LCY bond issuance in 2023 inched up to USD9.9 trillion from USD8.9 trillion in 2022. The region's y-o-y increase in issuance in 2023 was primarily driven by the PRC with total issuance of USD6.3 trillion, which was up from USD5.8 trillion in 2022 and comprised 63.9% of the annual regional total (**Figure 6**). In Q4 2023, LCY bond issuance in emerging East Asia totaled USD2.5 trillion, equivalent to 51.7% of issuance in the US during the quarter (USD4.8 trillion) and almost four times that of the EU-20 (USD0.7 trillion). During Q4 2023, the PRC accounted for 63.2% of total regional issuance, followed by ASEAN markets (21.2%); the Republic of Korea (9.3%); and Hong Kong, China (6.3%).

Figure 6: Local Currency Bond Issuance in Select Emerging East Asian Markets

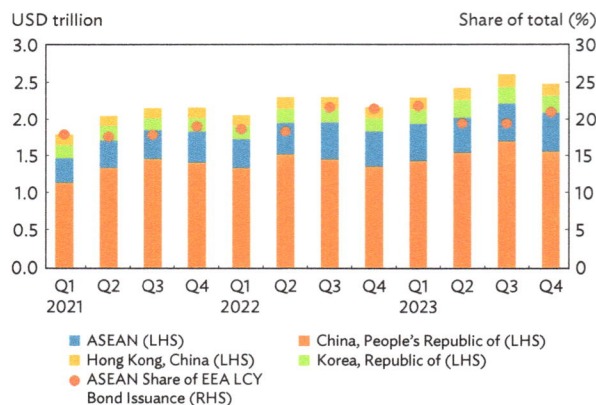

ASEAN = Association of Southeast Asian Nations, EEA = emerging East Asia, LCY = local currency, LHS = left-hand side, Q1 = first quarter, Q2 = second quarter, Q3 = third quarter, Q4 = fourth quarter, RHS = right-hand side, USD = United States dollar.
Notes:
1. ASEAN comprises the markets of Indonesia, Malaysia, the Philippines, Singapore, Thailand, and Viet Nam.
2. Figures were computed based on 31 December 2023 currency exchange rates and do not include currency effects.
Source: People's Republic of China (CEIC Data Company); Hong Kong, China (Hong Kong Monetary Authority); Indonesia (Bank Indonesia; Directorate General of Budget Financing and Risk Management, Ministry of Finance; and Indonesia Stock Exchange); Republic of Korea (Bank of Korea and KG Zeroin Corporation); Malaysia (Bank Negara Malaysia); Philippines (Bureau of the Treasury and Bloomberg LP); Singapore (Monetary Authority of Singapore and Bloomberg LP); Thailand (Bank of Thailand and Thai Bond Market Association); and Viet Nam (Vietnam Bond Market Association and Bloomberg LP).

Total LCY bond issuance in emerging East Asia declined 4.8% q-o-q in Q4 2023, a reversal from the 7.5% q-o-q increase in Q3 2023, driven by a contraction in government bond issuance. Issuance of government bonds fell 6.3% q-o-q to USD1.1 trillion in Q4 2023 as governments in the region had already fulfilled their borrowing requirements in the first 3 quarters of the year. However, despite the decline in total government bond issuance during the quarter, there were smaller volume of maturities in almost all markets, resulting in positive growth for government bonds outstanding in Q4 2023. All markets posted q-o-q issuance declines in Q4 2023, led by the PRC, which comprised 89.3% of the regional government bond total at the end of December (**Figure 7**). Issuance in the PRC fell 3.8% q-o-q in Q4 2023 due to reduced issuance of policy bank bonds and local government bonds, as most local government annual bond quotas had already been met by the end of Q3 2023. Government bonds issued in ASEAN markets; the Republic of Korea; and Hong Kong, China fell 15.3% q-o-q, 33.8% q-o-q, and 47.9% q-o-q, respectively. Meanwhile, issuance of central bank bonds in emerging East Asia rose 3.4% q-o-q, driven by higher issuance volumes in Singapore and Hong Kong, China.

Total corporate bond issuance fell 7.8% q-o-q to USD0.9 trillion from USD1.0 trillion in Q3 2023, dragged down by a contraction in the PRC. While five out of nine regional markets registered increased quarterly issuance in Q4 2023, regional corporate bond issuance growth was offset by the 13.4% q-o-q contraction in the PRC, which accounted for 72.7% of the region's quarterly total (**Table 2**). Contraction in corporate bond issuance in the PRC was partly due to the weakening property sector and its possible spillover to economic growth. On the other hand, corporate bond issuance rose in Q4 2023 in the Republic of Korea (21.4% q-o-q) and in ASEAN markets (5.3% q-o-q) on improving financial conditions driven by expectations of the ending of monetary tightening in both the US and regional markets.

A majority of Treasury bonds issued in emerging East Asia in Q4 2023 carried medium- to long-term tenors (**Figure 8a**). Around 53.2% of the region's Treasury bond issuance in Q4 2023 had tenors of over 5 years, which includes all issuance in the Philippines and Singapore, and more than 90% in Viet Nam (**Figure 8b**). Treasury bonds issued during the quarter had a size-weighted average tenor of 7.3 years, slightly higher than the average of 6.3 years in Q3 2023. For full-year 2023, the regional size-weighted tenor of Treasury bond issuance was 7.4 years, with ASEAN Treasury bonds having a much longer size-weighted tenor of 9.3 years.

Section 3. Bond Trading Activities

Turnover ratios in regional government bond markets trended slightly downward in most of ASEAN and in the Republic of Korea in 2023, but increased in the PRC; Hong Kong, China; and Viet Nam (**Figure 9**). In most regional bond markets, trading activities slightly eased toward the latter part of the year as government bond issuance wound down after frontloaded borrowing in earlier quarters. In markets such as the PRC and Viet Nam, improved bond trading activities were boosted by the monetary policy easing of their central banks to support economic activities amid a property sector downturn.

Similar to government bond markets, turnover ratios also declined in most emerging East Asian corporate bond markets in 2023 (**Figure 10**). The exceptions to this trend were the corporate bond markets of Indonesia and the Republic of Korea, where turnover ratios significantly increased during the year, particularly in Q4 2023. In Indonesia, increased trading activities were driven by the resurgence of corporate bond issuance in the second half of the year. A notable decline in turnover ratios was seen in the PRC due to dampened sentiment in corporate bonds over continued weakness in the domestic economy and credit concerns in the property market.

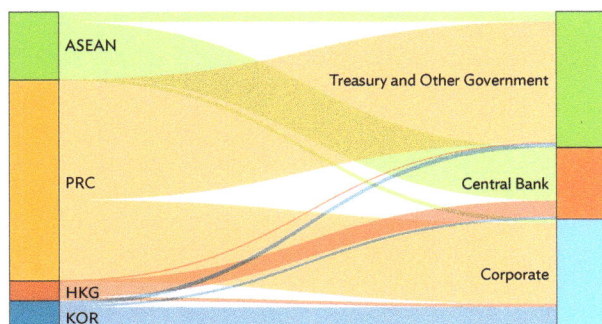

Figure 7: Local Currency Bond Issuance in Emerging East Asia by Economy and Type of Bond in the Fourth Quarter of 2023

ASEAN = Association of Southeast Asian Nations; HKG = Hong Kong, China; KOR = Republic of Korea; PRC = People's Republic of China.

Note: ASEAN comprises the markets of Indonesia, Malaysia, the Philippines, Singapore, Thailand, and Viet Nam.

Source: *AsianBondsOnline* calculations based on various local sources.

Table 2: Local-Currency-Denominated Bond Issuance

	Q4 2022		Q3 2023		Q4 2023		Growth Rate (%) Q4 2023	
	Amount (USD billion)	% share	Amount (USD billion)	% share	Amount (USD billion)	% share	q-o-q	y-o-y
China, People's Republic of								
Total	1,421	100.0	1,673	100.0	1,584	100.0	(7.9)	14.7
Treasury and Other Government	774	54.5	957	57.2	946	59.7	(3.8)	25.8
Central Bank	0	0.0	0	0.0	0	0.0	–	–
Corporate	647	45.5	716	43	638	40.3	(13.4)	1.4
Hong Kong, China								
Total	150	100.0	168	100.0	158	100.0	(6.3)	5.5
Treasury and Other Government	0.8	0.5	7	4.4	4	2.5	(47.9)	408.3
Government	124	82.9	127	75.6	129	81.9	1.6	4.2
Corporate	25	16.6	34	20	25	15.6	(26.8)	(0.7)
Indonesia								
Total	39	100.0	26	100.0	30	100.0	13.1	(24.0)
Treasury and Other Government	15	39.7	13	47.9	9	29.3	(30.8)	(44.0)
Central Bank	22	55.8	11	41.5	19	62.6	70.6	(14.8)
Corporate	2	4.5	3	11	2	8.1	(13.5)	38.6
Korea, Republic of								
Total	187	100.0	215	100.0	232	100.0	2.9	26.4
Treasury and Other Government	35	19.0	47	21.7	32	14.0	(33.8)	(6.8)
Central Bank	19	10.3	25	11.7	17	7.5	(34.0)	(7.7)
Corporate	132	70.7	143	66.5	182	78.5	21.4	40.3
Malaysia								
Total	27	100.0	37	100.0	34	100.0	(12.2)	29.4
Treasury and Other Government	10	37.7	12	32.6	10	29.1	(21.7)	0.0
Central Bank	0.3	1.0	16	42.3	14	41.4	(14.1)	5,233.3
Corporate	17	61.3	9	25.0	10	29.4	3.2	(37.8)
Philippines								
Total	39	100.0	42	100.0	41	100.0	(4.4)	5.5
Treasury and Other Government	7	19.1	10	24.6	8	19.0	(26.2)	4.8
Central Bank	29	75.0	31	73.7	32	77.8	0.9	9.5
Corporate	2	5.9	0.7	1.7	1	3.2	85.5	(42.4)
Singapore								
Total	279	100.0	324	100.0	352	100.0	4.9	24.0
Treasury and Other Government	28	9.9	35	10.8	35	9.8	(5.0)	23.2
Central Bank	250	89.4	288	88.9	316	89.8	6.0	24.5
Corporate	2	0.7	0.96	0.3	1	0.4	46.2	(27.2)
Thailand								
Total	64	100.0	61	100.0	58	100.0	(11.3)	(10.1)
Treasury and Other Government	18	28.1	15	24.0	14	24.7	(8.9)	(21.1)
Central Bank	31	49.4	33	54.0	30	52.2	(14.3)	(5.0)
Corporate	14	22.5	13	22.0	13	23.1	(6.7)	(7.8)
Viet Nam								
Total	23	100.0	9	100.0	16	100.0	81.6	(26.3)
Treasury and Other Government	4	19.3	3	33.0	2	10.3	(43.5)	(60.8)
Central Bank	18	79.9	4	42.6	11	66.6	184.2	(38.5)
Corporate	0.2	0.8	2	24.4	4	23.1	72.1	1,957.4
Emerging East Asia								
Total	2,229	100.0	2,556	100.0	2,505	100.0	(4.8)	14.4
Treasury and Other Government	893	40.1	1,099	43.0	1,059	42.3	(6.3)	21.6
Central Bank	494	22.2	535	20.9	568	22.7	3.4	14.2
Corporate	841	37.7	923	36.1	877	35.0	(7.8)	6.9
Japan								
Total	481	100.0	378	100.0	431	100.0	7.6	(3.7)
Treasury and Other Government	448	93.1	340	89.9	389	90.2	7.9	(6.7)
Central Bank	0	0.0	0	0.0	14	3.3	–	–
Corporate	33	6.9	38	10.1	28	6.5	(30.2)	(8.1)

( ) = negative, – = not applicable, Q3 = third quarter, Q4 = fourth quarter, q-o-q = quarter-on-quarter, USD = United States dollar, y-o-y = year-on-year.
Notes:
1. Data reflect gross bond issuance.
2. Bloomberg LP end-of-period local currency–USD rates are used.
3. Growth rates are calculated from a local currency base and do not include currency effects. For emerging East Asia, growth figures are based on 31 December 2023 currency exchange rates and do not include currency effects.

Source: People's Republic of China (CEIC Data Company); Hong Kong, China (Hong Kong Monetary Authority); Indonesia (Bank Indonesia, Directorate General of Budget Financing and Risk Management, Ministry of Finance; and Indonesia Stock Exchange); Republic of Korea (Bank of Korea and KG Zeroin Corporation); Malaysia (Bank Negara Malaysia); Philippines (Bureau of the Treasury and Bloomberg LP); Singapore (Monetary Authority of Singapore and Bloomberg LP); Thailand (Bank of Thailand and Thai Bond Market Association); Viet Nam (Vietnam Bond Market Association and Bloomberg LP); and Japan (Japan Securities Dealers Association).

Figure 8: Maturity Structure of Local Currency Treasury Bond Issuance in Emerging East Asia

a. Quarterly Maturity Structure
b. Maturity Structure by Market, Q4 2023

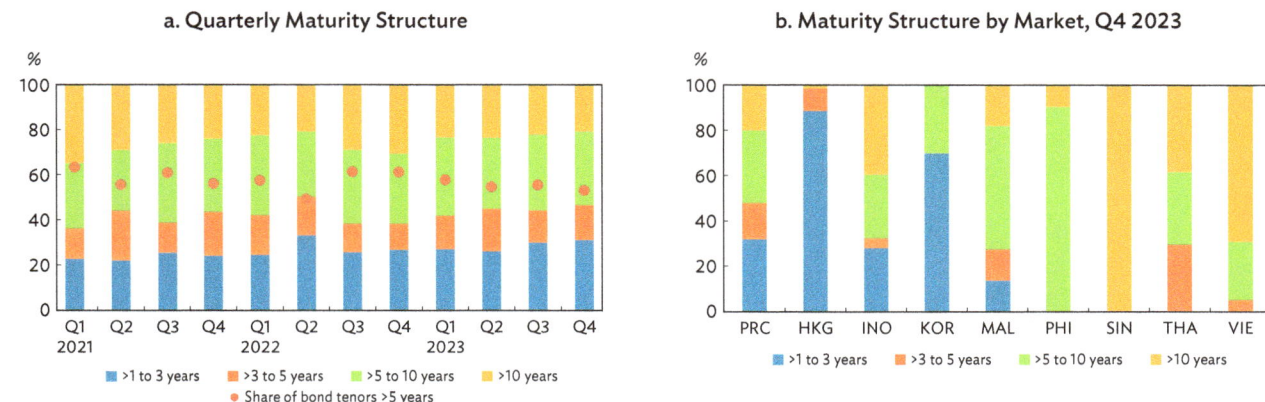

HKG = Hong Kong, China; INO = Indonesia; KOR = Republic of Korea; MAL = Malaysia; PHI = Philippines; PRC = People's Republic of China; Q1 = first quarter; Q2 = second quarter; Q3 = third quarter; Q4 = fourth quarter; SIN = Singapore; THA = Thailand; VIE = Viet Nam.

Notes:
1. Figures were computed based on 31 December 2023 currency exchange rates and do not include currency effects.
2. Treasury bonds are local-currency-denominated, fixed-income securities with maturities longer than 1 year and issued by the government.

Source: *AsianBondsOnline* calculations based on various local sources.

Figure 9: Local Currency Government Bond Turnover Ratios in Select Emerging East Asian Markets

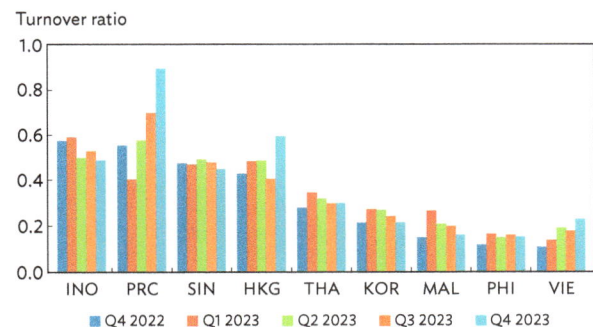

HKG = Hong Kong, China; INO = Indonesia; KOR = Republic of Korea; MAL = Malaysia; PHI = Philippines; PRC = People's Republic of China; Q1 = first quarter; Q2 = second quarter; Q3 = third quarter; Q4 = fourth quarter; SIN = Singapore; THA = Thailand; VIE = Viet Nam.

Note: Turnover ratios are calculated as local currency trading volume (sales amount only) divided by average local currency value of outstanding bonds during each 3-month period.

Sources: People's Republic of China (CEIC Data Company); Hong Kong, China (Hong Kong Monetary Authority); Indonesia (Indonesia Stock Exchange); Republic of Korea (Bank of Korea and KG Zeroin Corporation); Malaysia (BankNegara Malaysia); Philippines (Philippine Dealing and Exchange Corporation); Singapore (Monetary Authority of Singapore and Singapore Government Securities); Thailand (Bank of Thailand and Thai Bond Market Association); and Viet Nam (Vietnam Ministry of Finance).

Figure 10: Local Currency Corporate Bond Turnover Ratios in Select Emerging East Asian Markets

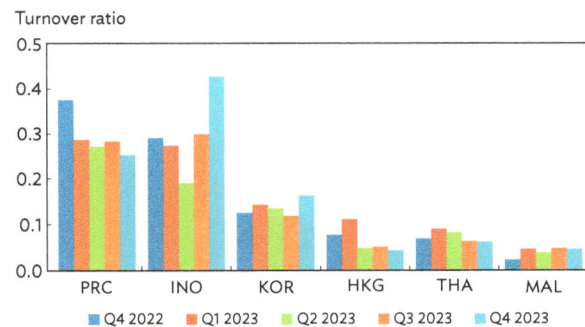

HKG = Hong Kong, China; INO = Indonesia; KOR = Republic of Korea; MAL = Malaysia; PHI = Philippines; PRC = People's Republic of China; Q1 = first quarter; Q2 = second quarter; Q3 = third quarter; Q4 = fourth quarter; THA = Thailand.

Note: Turnover ratios are calculated as local currency trading volume (sales amount only) divided by the average local currency value of outstanding bonds during each 3-month period.

Sources: People's Republic of China (CEIC Data Company); Hong Kong, China (Hong Kong Monetary Authority); Indonesia (Indonesia Stock Exchange); Republic of Korea (Bank of Korea and KG Zeroin Corporation); Malaysia (Bank Negara Malaysia); and Thailand (Bank of Thailand and Thai Bond Market Association).

Section 4. Intra-Regional Bond Issuance

Intra-regional bond issuance in emerging East Asia totaled USD9.4 billion in Q4 2023, a contraction of 33.4% q-o-q from USD14.1 billion in Q3 2023 (**Figure 11**).[4] Compared to the same period in 2022, the region's total intra-regional bond issuance dropped 19.8% from USD11.7 billion. The contraction in intra-regional bond issuance in Q4 2023 was mainly driven by a significant decline in issuance from the Republic of Korea to USD0.5 billion from USD6.3 billion in Q3 2023. The decline in the Republic of Korea's intra-regional bond issuance offset increased issuance in Hong Kong, China; Malaysia; the Lao People's Democratic Republic; and Singapore. Hong Kong, China remained the largest issuer of intra-regional bonds in emerging East Asia in Q4 2023 at USD8.0 billion, accounting for 84.6% of the regional total. Singapore was the region's second-largest issuer of intra-regional bonds during the quarter, with issuance volume increasing almost threefold to USD0.5 billion from USD0.2 billion in Q3 2023, accounting for 5.4% of the regional total. The Republic of Korea's total intra-regional bond issuance accounted for 5.3% of the regional total, making it the third-largest issuer of intra-regional bonds during the quarter. Malaysia and the Lao People's Democratic Republic increased their intra-regional bond issuance in Q4 2023 to USD0.3 billion and

USD0.1 billion, respectively, with regional shares of 3.6% and 1.1%. For full-year 2023, total intra-regional bond issuance in emerging East Asia reached USD48.2 billion, posting an annual increase of 38.5% from USD34.8 billion in 2022.

In Q4 2023, intra-regional bond issuance was dominated by CNY-denominated bonds and issuances from the transportation sector. CNY-denominated issuance totaled USD8.5 billion during the quarter, accounting for 89.9% of the regional aggregate (**Figure 12**). CNY-denominated issuance came from Hong Kong, China; the Republic of Korea; and Singapore. Issuance denominated in Hong Kong dollars, Singapore dollars, and Thai baht collectively accounted for 10.1% of total intra-regional issuance in emerging East Asia in Q4 2023. By sector, issuance from transportation firms reached USD3.0 billion, an increase of more than twofold from the previous quarter's USD1.4 billion. The transportation sector comprised 31.9% of the regional total in Q4 2023, surpassing the financial sector, the second-largest issuer of intra-regional bonds, with USD2.1 billion in issuance and a regional share of 22.7%. The utilities and industrial sectors, whose issuances increased during the quarter, were the third- and fourth-largest sources of intra-regional bonds in Q4 2023, respectively, accounting for 17.9% and 12.9%, of the regional total.

Figure 11: Intra-Regional Bond Issuance in Select Emerging East Asian Economies

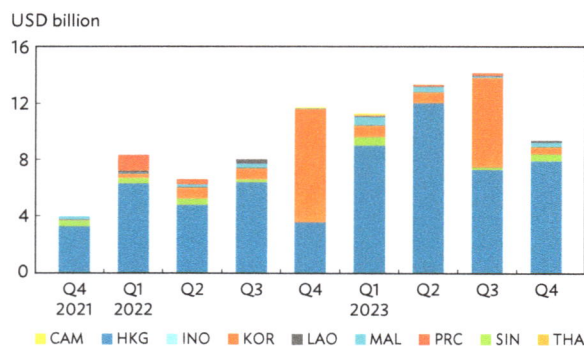

CAM = Cambodia; HKG = Hong Kong, China; INO = Indonesia; KOR = Republic of Korea; LAO = Lao People's Democratic Republic; MAL = Malaysia; PRC = People's Republic of China; Q1 = first quarter; Q2 = second quarter; Q3 = third quarter; Q4 = fourth quarter; SIN = Singapore; THA = Thailand; USD = United States dollar.
Source: *AsianBondsOnline* calculations based on Bloomberg LP data.

Figure 12: Intra-Regional Bond Issuance in Emerging East Asia by Economy, Currency, and Sector in the Fourth Quarter of 2023

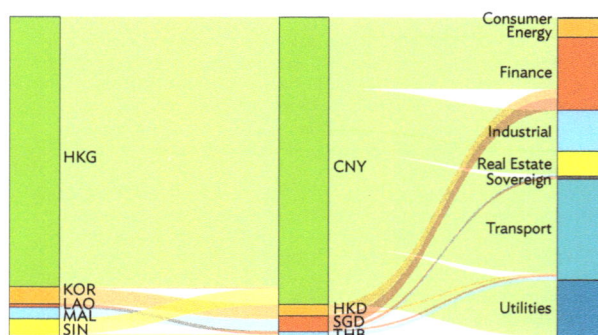

CNY = Chinese yuan; HKD = Hong Kong dollar; HKG = Hong Kong, China; KOR = Republic of Korea; LAO = Lao People's Democratic Republic; MAL = Malaysia; SGD = Singapore dollar; SIN = Singapore; THB = Thai baht.
Source: *AsianBondsOnline* calculations based on Bloomberg LP data.

---

[4] Intra-regional bond issuance is defined as emerging East Asian bond issuance denominated in a regional currency excluding the issuer's home currency.

Section 5. G3 Currency Bond Issuance

ASEAN markets witnessed a rapid expansion in G3 currency bond issuance in Q4 2023. Emerging East Asia's issuance of G3 currency bonds in Q4 2023 amounted to USD45.3 billion, up 9.2% from the USD41.5 billion recorded in Q3 2023 (**Figure 13**). The PRC was the largest G3 currency bond issuer in emerging East Asia in Q4 2023 with total issuance of USD24.0 billion, accounting for 52.9% of the regional total. ASEAN markets' G3 currency bond issuance soared 58.6% q-o-q in Q4 2023, reaching USD10.1 billion and accounting for 22.4% of the regional total (**Figure 14**). The biggest issuers of G3 currency bonds during the quarter among ASEAN markets were Indonesia and Malaysia, which issued USD3.2 billion and USD2.8 billion, respectively. The Philippines, whose last G3 currency bond issuance was in the first quarter of 2023, returned to the market in Q4 2023 with its first issuance of a

USD-denominated government *sukuk* (Islamic bond) in December amounting to USD1.0 billion. The issuance was part of government efforts to support the development of Islamic banking and finance in the Philippines. In November, Vingroup issued Viet Nam's only G3 currency bond in 2023. G3 currency bonds issued in emerging East Asia amounted to USD185.5 billion in 2023, down from USD223.3 billion in the previous year due to higher interest rates.

Section 6. Yield Curve Movements

Due to expectations of the end of monetary tightening, bond yields fell for nearly all tenors in almost all emerging East Asian markets from 1 December 2023 to 29 February 2024 (Figure 15). The decline in yields was largely driven by (i) expectations that the US Federal Reserve would begin cutting its policy rates in 2024, and (ii) moderating inflation across the region.

Figure 13: Monthly G3 Currency Bond Issuance in Select Emerging East Asian Markets

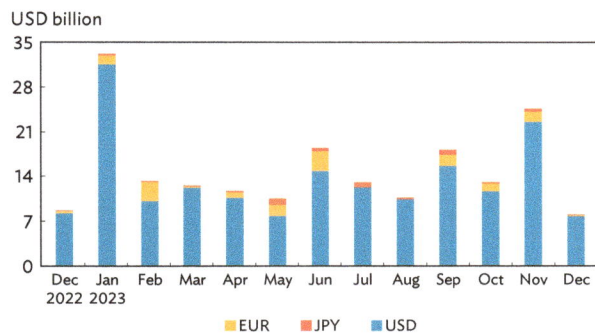

EUR = euro, JPY = Japanese yen, USD = United States dollar.
Notes:
1. Emerging East Asia is defined to include member states of the Association of Southeast Asian Nations (ASEAN) plus the People's Republic of China; Hong Kong, China; and the Republic of Korea.
2. G3 currency bonds are denominated in either euros, Japanese yen, or United States dollars.
3. Figures were computed based on 31 December 2023 currency exchange rates and do not include currency effects.
Source: *AsianBondsOnline* calculations based on Bloomberg LP data.

Figure 14: G3 Currency Bond Issuance in Emerging East Asia in the Fourth Quarter of 2023

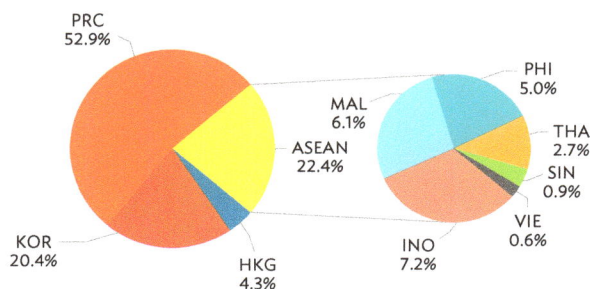

ASEAN = Association of Southeast Asian Nations; HKG = Hong Kong, China; INO = Indonesia; KOR = Republic of Korea; MAL = Malaysia; PHI = Philippines; PRC = People's Republic of China; SIN = Singapore; THA = Thailand; VIE = Viet Nam.
Note: G3 currency bonds are denominated in either euros, Japanese yen, or United States dollars.
Source: *AsianBondsOnline* calculations based on Bloomberg LP data.

Figure 15: Benchmark Yield Curves—Local Currency Government Bonds

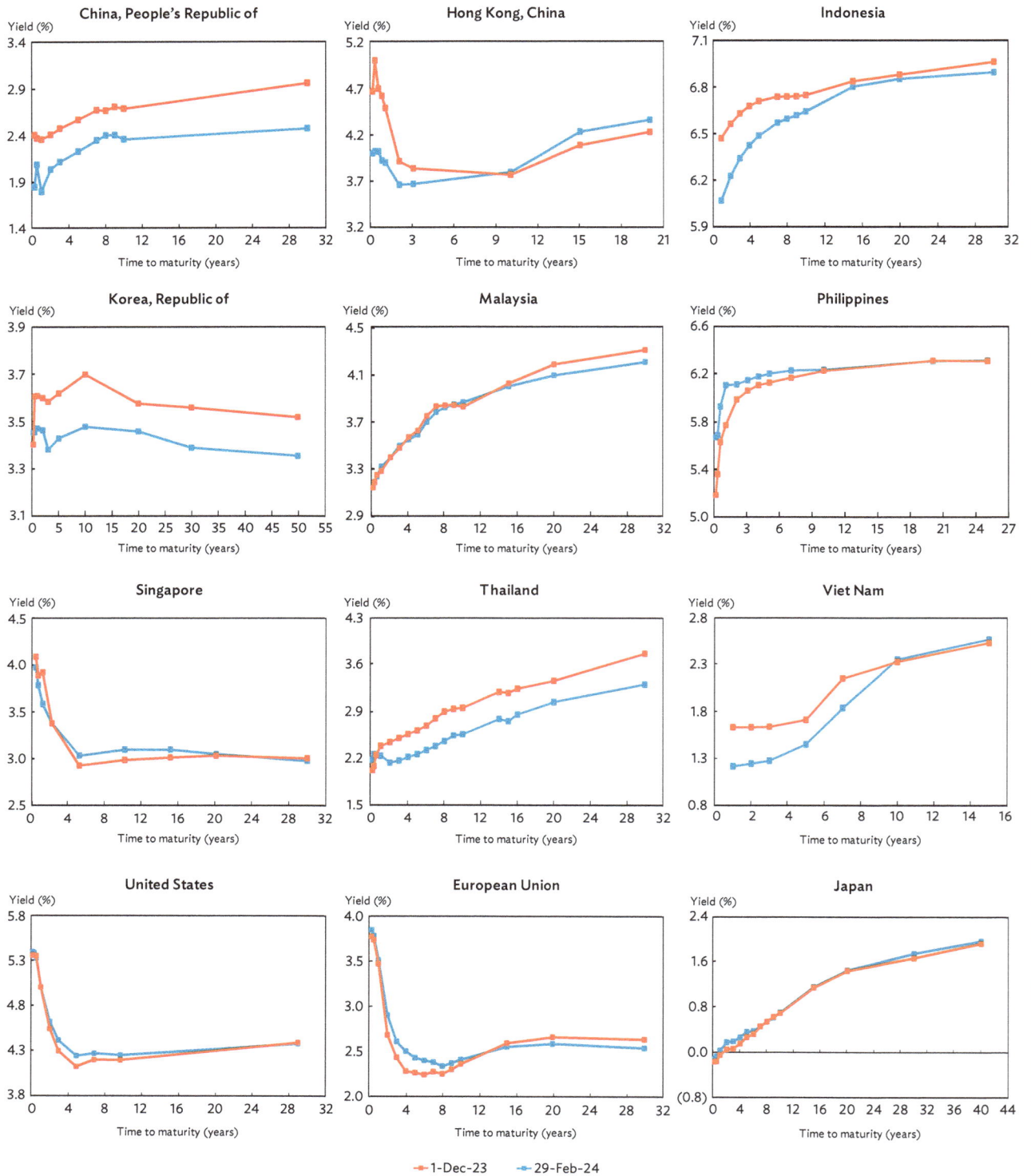

( ) = negative.
Sources: Based on data from Bloomberg LP and Thai Bond Market Association.

Recent Developments in ASEAN+3 Sustainable Bond Markets

The sustainable bond market in ASEAN+3 reached a size of USD798.7 billion at the end of 2023, expanding more than sevenfold from USD109.7 billion in 2017.[5] The expansion reflected average annual growth of 43.0% over the past 7 years, which is lower than the global sustainable bond market's average annual growth rate of 52.2% over the same period (**Figure 16**). In 2023, however, the ASEAN+3 sustainable bond market grew 29.3% year-on-year (y-o-y), posting a faster annual rate of expansion than the global sustainable bond market (21.0%) and the European Union (EU-20) market (21.0%). Rapid expansion in 2023 pushed up ASEAN+3's share of total global sustainable bonds outstanding (USD4.0 trillion) to 20.1% from 18.8% in 2022, although this still trailed the EU-20's share of 37.7%. Despite the rapid expansion, sustainable bonds outstanding in ASEAN+3 only accounted for 2.1% of the region's general bond market at the end of 2023, which was much lower than the corresponding share of 6.9% in the EU-20.

Green bonds, corporate bonds, and local currency (LCY) bonds are the most prevalent instruments in ASEAN+3 sustainable bond markets. Figure 17 presents the profile of outstanding sustainable bonds in ASEAN+3. Green bonds are the most common bond type, accounting for 63.8% of the ASEAN+3 total, followed by social bonds (17.2%). The People's Republic of China (PRC) has the largest sustainable bond market in ASEAN+3, accounting for 43.4% of the region's total sustainable bonds outstanding at the end of 2023. However, this was lower than the PRC's share of 54.3% in the ASEAN+3 general bond market. ASEAN markets accounted for 9.1% of the regional total, higher than ASEAN's share of 6.1% in the region's general bond market. Around 74% of outstanding sustainable bonds in

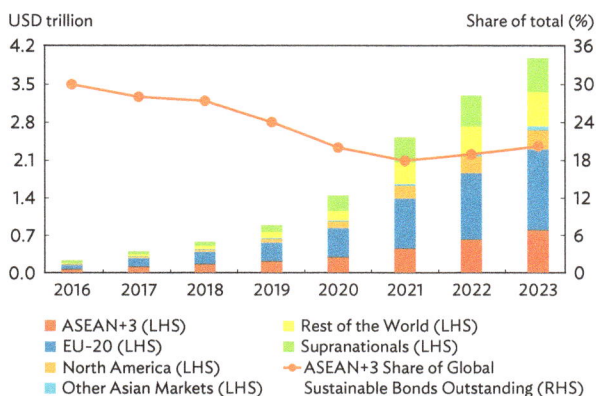

Figure 16: Global Sustainable Bonds Outstanding

ASEAN+3 = Association of Southeast Asian Nations plus the People's Republic of China; Hong Kong, China; Japan; and the Republic of Korea; EU = European Union; LHS = left-hand side; RHS = right-hand side; USD = United States dollar.

Notes:
1. EU-20 includes EU member markets Austria, Belgium, Croatia, Cyprus, Estonia, Finland, France, Germany, Greece, Ireland, Italy, Latvia, Lithuania, Luxembourg, Malta, the Netherlands, Portugal, Slovakia, Slovenia, and Spain.
2. Data include both local currency and foreign currency issues.

Source: *AsianBondsOnline* calculations based on Bloomberg LP data.

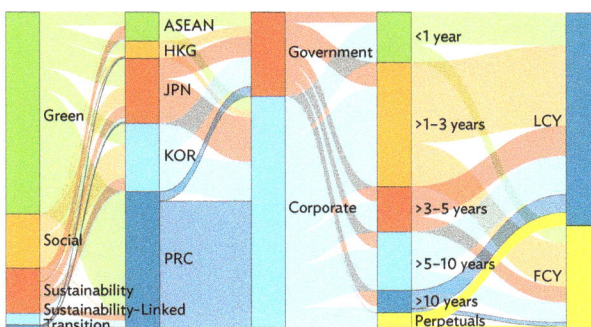

Figure 17: Market Profile of Outstanding ASEAN+3 Sustainable Bonds at the End of December 2023

ASEAN = Association of Southeast Asian Nations; FCY = foreign currency; HKG = Hong Kong, China; JPN = Japan; KOR = Republic of Korea; LCY = local currency; PRC = People's Republic of China.

Notes:
1. ASEAN+3 is defined to include member states of the Association of Southeast Asian Nations (ASEAN) plus the People's Republic of China; Hong Kong, China; Japan; and the Republic of Korea.
2. ASEAN comprises the markets of Cambodia, Indonesia, the Lao People's Democratic Republic, Malaysia, the Philippines, Singapore, Thailand, and Viet Nam.

Source: *AsianBondsOnline* calculations based on Bloomberg LP data.

---

[5] ASEAN+3 is defined to include member states of the Association of Southeast Asian Nations (ASEAN) plus the People's Republic of China; Hong Kong, China; Japan; and the Republic of Korea.

ASEAN+3 at the end of 2023 were issued by the private sector, this contrasts with the private sector's much smaller share of 25.8% in the ASEAN+3 general bond market. While ASEAN+3 sustainable bonds outstanding at the end of 2023 were mostly issued in domestic currencies (67.2%), this was well below the LCY bond share of 94.8% in the ASEAN+3 general bond market. In the EU-20, the share of LCY bonds among total outstanding sustainable bonds (89.9%) was similar to the corresponding LCY share in the EU-20 general bond market (90.6%).

ASEAN markets have a relatively high share of long-term sustainable bonds due to public sector issuance. As shown in **Figure 18**, 69.6% of outstanding ASEAN+3 sustainable bonds at the end of 2023 carried a tenor of 5 years or less. The size-weighted average tenor of outstanding ASEAN+3 sustainable bonds was 4.5 years. This contrasts with the corresponding average tenor of 8.7 years in the EU-20, where only 38.8% of outstanding sustainable bonds carried a tenor of 5 years or less at the end of 2023. However, in ASEAN markets, 68.6% of outstanding sustainable bonds had a tenor longer than 5 years at the end of December (**Figure 19**), which was higher than the corresponding shares in the PRC (20.9%), Japan (43.1%), and the Republic of Korea (20.3%), as well as the EU-20 (61.2%). Longer average

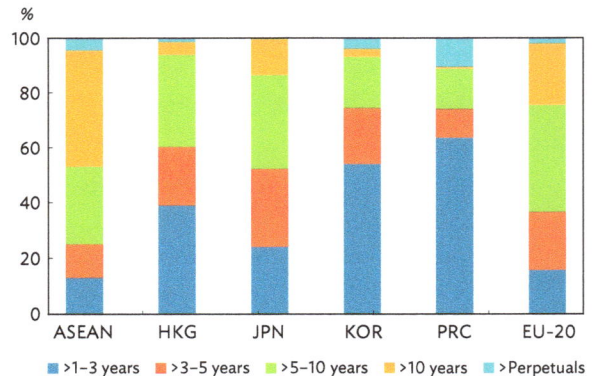

Figure 19: Maturity Profiles of ASEAN+3 and EU-20 Sustainable Bonds Outstanding in 2023

ASEAN+3 = Association of Southeast Asian Nations plus the People's Republic of China; Hong Kong, China; Japan; and the Republic of Korea; EU-20 = European Union.
Notes:
1. The EU-20 includes EU member markets Austria, Belgium, Croatia, Cyprus, Estonia, Finland, France, Germany, Greece, Ireland, Italy, Latvia, Lithuania, Luxembourg, Malta, the Netherlands, Portugal, Slovakia, Slovenia, and Spain.
2. Data include both local currency and foreign currency issues.
Source: *AsianBondsOnline* computations based on Bloomberg LP data.

tenors in ASEAN markets are being driven by public sector issuances, which accounted for 49.1% of ASEAN sustainable bonds outstanding at the end of 2023, compared with 26.5% in the ASEAN+3 sustainable bond market. In ASEAN markets, the size-weighted average tenor of sustainable bonds issued in the public sector is 15.9 years, which is much higher than the corresponding average of 6.0 years for sustainable bonds issued in the private sector. This is also the case in the ASEAN+3 sustainable bond market, where the size-weighted average tenor of public sector sustainable bonds outstanding is 6.9 years, while the corresponding figure for the private sector is only 3.6 years.

Sustainable bond issuance in ASEAN+3 totaled USD242.2 billion in 2023, just behind the EU-20's USD288.3 billion. Due to higher interest rates, global sustainable bond issuance declined from USD896.1 billion in 2022 to USD846.2 billion in 2023. While issuance in ASEAN+3 declined by 1.4% y-o-y, it still outperformed issuance growth in the EU-20, where a 7.5% y-o-y contraction was recorded. As a result, ASEAN+3's share of global sustainable bond issuance inched up to 28.6% in 2023 from 27.4% a year earlier (**Figure 20**). Issuance of all sustainable bond types in ASEAN+3 posted declines in 2023 except for social bonds, which rose 27.5% y-o-y. The robust issuance of social bonds in the region was largely supported by Japan and the Republic of Korea. In 2023, some large social bond issuances from Japan

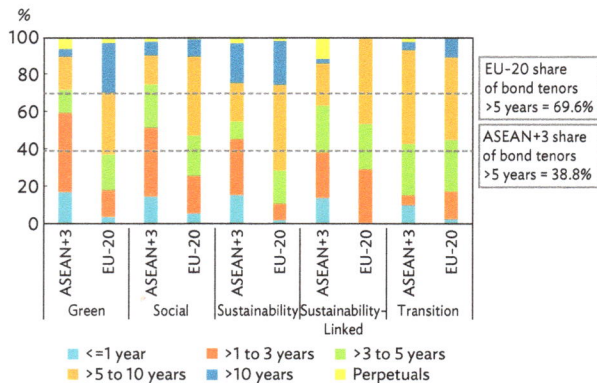

Figure 18: Maturity Profiles of ASEAN+3 and EU-20 Sustainable Bonds Outstanding by Type of Bond at the End of December 2023

ASEAN+3 = Association of Southeast Asian Nations plus the People's Republic of China; Hong Kong, China; Japan; and the Republic of Korea; EU = European Union.
Notes:
1. EU-20 includes EU member markets Austria, Belgium, Croatia, Cyprus, Estonia, Finland, France, Germany, Greece, Ireland, Italy, Latvia, Lithuania, Luxembourg, Malta, the Netherlands, Portugal, Slovakia, Slovenia, and Spain.
2. Data include both local currency and foreign currency issues.
Source: *AsianBondsOnline* calculations based on Bloomberg LP data.

Figure 20: ASEAN+3 Sustainable Bond Issuance and Share of the Global Total

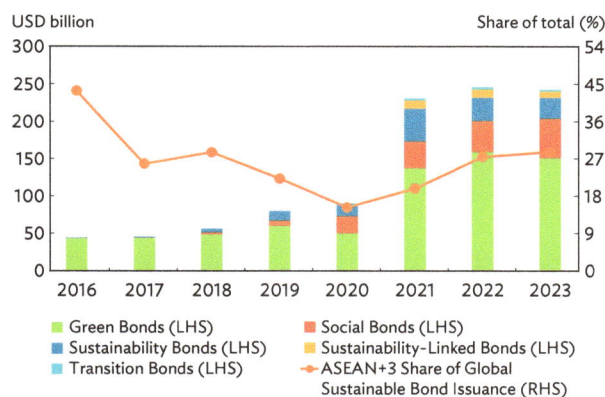

ASEAN+3 = Association of Southeast Asian Nations plus the People's Republic of China; Hong Kong, China; Japan; and the Republic of Korea; LHS = left-hand side; RHS = right-hand side; USD = United States dollar.

Note: Data include both local currency and foreign currency issues.

Source: *AsianBondsOnline* calculations based on Bloomberg LP data.

Figure 21: Market Profile of ASEAN+3 Sustainable Bond Issuance in 2023

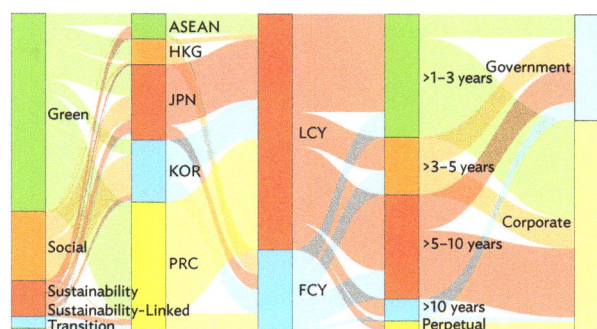

ASEAN = Association of Southeast Asian Nations; FCY = foreign currency; HKG = Hong Kong, China; JPN = Japan; KOR = Republic of Korea; LCY = local currency; PRC = People's Republic of China.

Notes:
1. ASEAN+3 is defined to include member states of ASEAN plus the People's Republic of China; Hong Kong, China; Japan; and the Republic of Korea.
2. ASEAN comprises the markets of Indonesia, Malaysia, the Philippines, Singapore, Thailand, and Viet Nam.

Source: *AsianBondsOnline* calculations based on Bloomberg LP data.

and the Republic of Korea included Japan Expressway Holding and Debt Repayment Agency (USD9.4 billion), West-Nippon Expressway Company (USD3.3 billion), Korea Housing Finance Corporation (USD8.0 billion), and Korea SMEs and Startups Agency (USD3.4 billion).

The majority of sustainable bond issuance in ASEAN+3 in 2023 was LCY-denominated, carried a short tenor, and came from the private sector. In 2023, 56.9% of sustainable bonds issued in the region carried maturities of 5 years or less, including 38.6% with maturities of 3 years or less (**Figure 21**). Sustainable bond issuances in ASEAN+3 in 2023 had a size-weighted average tenor of 6.2 years, which was below the EU-20's corresponding 8.8 years and the ASEAN+3 general bond market's 8.4 years. Similarly, in ASEAN markets, 84.9% of sustainable bonds issued in 2023 carried a longer tenor of more than 5 years. While 74.3% of ASEAN+3 sustainable bond issuance was LCY-denominated in 2023, this was less than the corresponding LCY issuance shares of 88.9% in the EU-20 sustainable bond market and 96.4% in the ASEAN+3 general bond market. In 2023, regional sustainable bond markets with the highest LCY issuance shares were the PRC (86.4%) and ASEAN markets (80.6%). In ASEAN, the relatively high share of LCY sustainable bond issuance was mostly driven by the public sector. In ASEAN markets, 61.2% of LCY-denominated sustainable bond issuance was from the public sector, while the corresponding share was only 38.8% for the private sector. In ASEAN+3, the private sector accounted

for 66.7% of overall sustainable bond issuance in 2023, in contrast to the private sector's much smaller share of 29.6% in the general bond market. Public sector issuances were most prevalent in the social bond segment in 2023, accounting for 61.6% of regional social bond issuance (**Figure 22**).

Figure 22: ASEAN+3 Sustainable Bond Issuance by Industry Sector in 2023

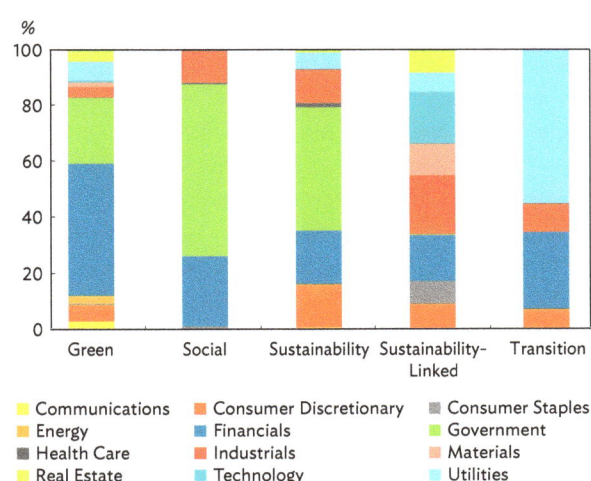

ASEAN = Association of Southeast Asian Nations.

Notes:
1. ASEAN+3 is defined to include member states of the Association of Southeast Asian Nations (ASEAN) plus the People's Republic of China; Hong Kong, China; Japan; and the Republic of Korea.
2. Data include both local currency and foreign currency issues.

Source: *AsianBondsOnline* computations based on Bloomberg LP data.

Policy and Regulatory Developments

People's Republic of China

People's Bank of China Cuts Reserve Requirement Ratio

On 24 January, the People's Bank of China (PBOC) announced a reduction in the reserve requirement ratio of financial institutions by 50 basis points, effective 5 February. The central bank estimated that the move will result in an average reserve requirement ratio of 7.0% for financial institutions. The PBOC also reduced the central bank lending rate for loans to support rural development and loans to micro and small businesses, as well as the discount rate, by 25 basis points.

Hong Kong, China

Hong Kong Monetary Authority and People's Bank of China Announce Measures to Promote Financial Cooperation

On 24 January, the Hong Kong Monetary Authority and the PBOC jointly announced six new policy measures to deepen financial cooperation between the markets of Hong Kong, China and the People's Republic of China (PRC). Three of the measures are linked to bond markets. One of the measures will allow bonds issued by the Ministry of Finance and policy banks of the PRC to be used as eligible collateral for the renminbi liquidity arrangement of the Hong Kong Monetary Authority. Another measure will open the domestic repurchase agreement market to foreign institutional investors who already have access to the China Interbank Bond Market. Also included is a measure that will promote cross-boundary credit referencing to facilitate corporates' cross-boundary financing activities. Collectively, these measures will enhance connectivity and expand foreign investors' access to the bond markets of Hong Kong, China and the PRC.

Indonesia

Financial Services Authority Issues Regulation on the Issuance of Sustainable Debt Securities

In October, the Financial Services Authority (Otoritas Jasa Keuangan) issued Regulation 18/2023 governing the issuance process and requirements for sustainable debt securities. With the new regulation, the range of sustainable debt securities was expanded to include all types of sustainable securities (green, social, sustainability, and sustainability-linked), applying to both conventional and *sukuk* (Islamic bond) issues. It also covers both publicly issued debt securities and private placements. Regulation 18/2023 details issuance requirements for sustainable debt securities that are based on international standards and best practices established by institutions such as the International Capital Markets Association, Association of Southeast Asian Nations Capital Markets Forum, and Securities Commission Malaysia.

Republic of Korea

Ministry of Economy and Finance Introduces 30-Year Government Bond Futures

On 19 February, the Ministry of Economy and Finance announced the introduction of the 30-year government bond futures to help investors manage interest rate risk and to further deepen long-term government bond trading and issuance. The ministry also announced support from the Korea Exchange in terms of futures settlement, including temporary exemption from transaction fees and the inclusion of futures in the market-maker system. Moreover, the maximum volume for the absorption of off-the-run Treasuries and the supply of new on-the-run 30-year Treasuries in the exchange will be increased to KRW500 billion per month to support the liquidity of 30-year Treasury bonds.

Malaysia

Bank Negara Malaysia Defends Depreciation of the Ringgit

On 20 February, the Bank Negara Malaysia addressed investor concerns over the Malaysian ringgit's value after it fell to its lowest level against the United States dollar since the 1997/98 Asian financial crisis. The central bank assured financial market participants that Malaysia's economy continued to enjoy strong fundamentals and a positive outlook despite the depreciation of the currency. The falling ringgit is mainly being affected by external factors such as reduced exports due to the PRC's sluggish economic growth and shifting expectations of the pace of monetary tightening by the United States Federal Reserve. According to the central bank, analysts expect the Malaysian ringgit to rebound in 2024.

Philippines

The Philippines Launches Its Maiden Tokenized Bonds

On 22 November, the Bureau of the Treasury (BTr) raised PHP15.0 billion from the sale of its first Tokenized Treasury Bonds (TTBs) with a coupon rate of 6.5% and a tenor of 1 year. The TTBs were offered to qualified institutional investors in minimum denominations of PHP10 million and increments of PHP1 million thereafter. For this program, the BTr implemented a dual registry structure, where TTBs were issued in scripless form through the National Registry of Scripless Securities, which serves as the primary registry, and in tokenized format through the Distributed Ledger Technology Registry. The BTr's issuance of TTBs aim to promote greater financial inclusion and modernization of financial platforms through digital technology. The Government of the Philippines is planning to expand this project to retail investors in the future.

The Philippines Issues its First Dollar Islamic Bonds

The Government of the Philippines tapped the global Islamic financial market for the first time through its maiden issuance of 5.5-year USD-denominated *sukuk* with a profit rate of 5.045%. The government successfully raised USD1.0 billion from its offering in late November and settled the transaction on 6 December. The maiden issuance of *sukuk* aims to further develop Islamic banking and finance in the Philippines in order to diversify the government's global investor base across the Middle East. In addition, this issuance seeks to establish an active and liquid reference curve for the *sukuk* market for future issuers. The net proceeds of the bond completed the government's external commercial funding requirements for 2023 and will be used for general purposes, including but not limited to the government's budgetary support.

Singapore

Monetary Authority of Singapore Launches the Singapore Sustainable Finance Association

On 24 January, the Monetary Authority of Singapore launched the Singapore Sustainable Finance Association to ensure that Singapore remained the leading center for Asia's sustainable finance. The association is responsible for setting standards that can be a model for best industry practices. It also has the capability to bring together financial institutions and industry experts to identify challenges faced by groups needing financing for their sustainability projects. Lastly, the Singapore Sustainable Finance Association will lead capacity building in the sustainable finance market through educational courses.

Thailand

The Government of Thailand Approves Additional Borrowing for Fiscal Year 2024

On 13 February, the Government of Thailand approved an additional THB560 billion in new borrowing for fiscal year (FY) 2024, raising the amount allotted for new borrowing to more than THB754 billion. The public debt management plan was adjusted to THB2.0 trillion, up from THB1.62 trillion, to offset the budget deficit for FY 2024 and manage the Treasury reserve's liquidity. The adjustment brought the public debt-to-gross-domestic-product ratio to 61.3%, which is within the public debt ceiling of 70.0%. Approval and disbursement of the FY 2024 budget, which was supposed to start on 1 October 2023, has faced delays due to the transition to the new government.

Viet Nam

Viet Nam to Borrow VND676.1 Trillion in 2024

The Government of Viet Nam plans to borrow VND676.1 trillion in 2024 to cover the budget deficit, service existing debts, and provide additional loans. The planned borrowing is VND55.0 trillion higher than the amount that was previously approved by the National Assembly and VND71.7 trillion higher than total borrowing in 2023. The proposed borrowing comprises bond sales, official development assistance, and foreign preferential loans. Under this borrowing plan, Viet Nam's public debt is projected to be around 40% of gross domestic product at the end of 2024, while government and foreign debt will be around 38% and 39%, respectively. All of these percentages are below the debt ceiling rate of 60% that was set out by the National Assembly.

Environmental, Social, and Governance Performance and Its Financial Impacts: A Comparative Analysis of Companies in Asia

The global landscape for sustainable investments has witnessed substantial growth, with assets reported by the Global Sustainable Investment Alliance increasing from USD22.8 trillion in 2016 to USD35.3 trillion in 2020. Institutional investors, managing a total of USD98.4 trillion in assets, have designated more than one-third of these as environmental, social, and governance (ESG) investments. Notably, the Principles for Responsible Investment, a United Nations-supported international organization that encourages investors to take more responsibility with their investments, had garnered over 4,900 signatory organizations, representing a total of approximately USD121 trillion in managed assets, as of March 2022. The expansion of ESG investments has been particularly pronounced in the United States and Europe, where the number of signatories far surpasses those in Asia, emphasizing the growing global momentum toward responsible and sustainable investing.

ESG performance, which is the key factor contributing to ESG investment decisions, mainly refers to the evaluations provided by major ESG raters in the global market. However, current ESG ratings are criticized for their lack of commensurability, which can result in a misunderstanding of ESG practices and thereby confuse investment decisions. Furthermore, cultural contexts, such as the characteristics of individual institutions and the level of regional sustainability, play an important role in determining ESG performance and its financial impacts. To clarify these issues, this study delves into the world of ESG ratings provided by six major global rating agencies to compare ESG rating components at the firm level and

investigate the effects of market-specific attributes on ESG performance. The goal is to offer practical insights by empirically showcasing differences in ESG performance and financial impacts, with a special focus on companies in Asia.

The study reveals notable disparities in ESG scores across various raters, potentially leading to divergent interpretations when making investment decisions. The inconsistencies among ESG ratings are due to differences in the evaluated ESG components and the subjective–objective nature of the assessment procedures (**Figure 23a**). As a result, there is low correlation among scores given by the major ESG raters (**Figure 23b**).

While there is a lack of commensurability in ESG rating metrics, these ratings better reflect consensus at the market level. For example, the average ESG performance of firms in European economies exceeds that of their counterparts in Asian economies (**Figure 24**).

The financial implications of ESG practices vary across markets (**Figure 25**). Some Southeast Asian enterprises tend to see a higher correlation between ESG performance and financial performance, while businesses in developed economies and many other developing Asian economies see less correlation between implementing ESG strategies and companies' earnings and profitability. Considering the nature of ESG practices in improving corporate sustainability in the long term (**Figure 25b**), the financial impacts on firm value, proxied by Tobin's Q, are much more significant than short-term profitability (**Figure 25a**), captured by return on assets.

This note was written by Shunsuke Managi, distinguished professor at Kyushu University, and Jun Xie and Kenichi Yoshida of the Urban Institute. This note is a nontechnical summary based on a working paper titled "ESG Performance and Financial Impacts: Comparative Analysis of Companies in Asia."

Figure 23: Inconsistent Assessment Items across Environmental, Social, and Governance Raters

(a)

ESG

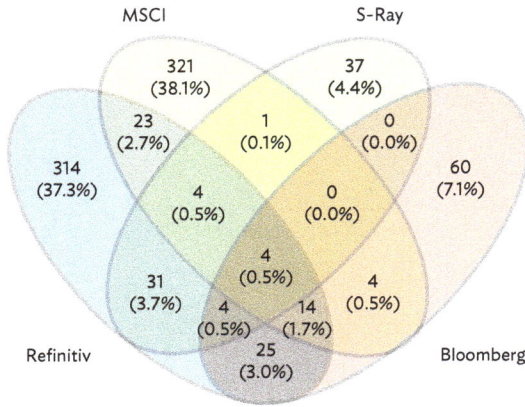

Environmental

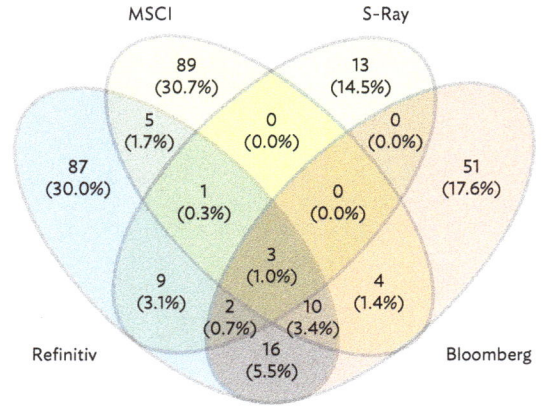

Social

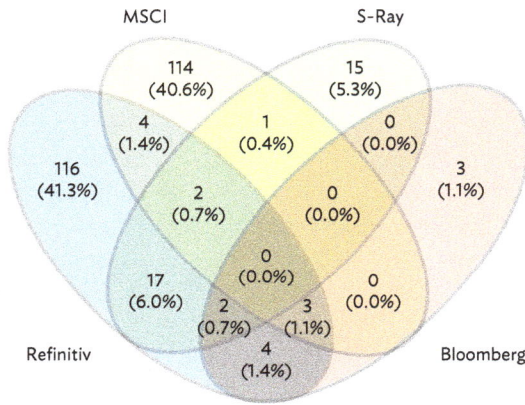

Governance

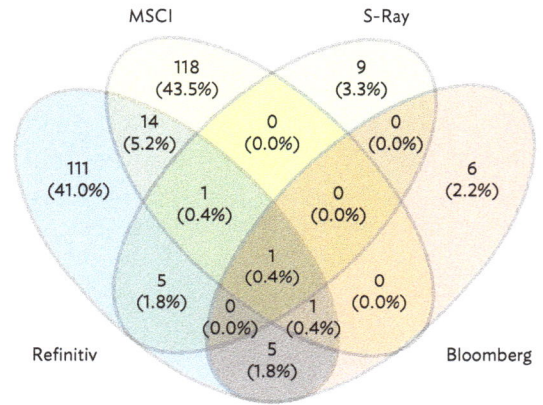

(b)

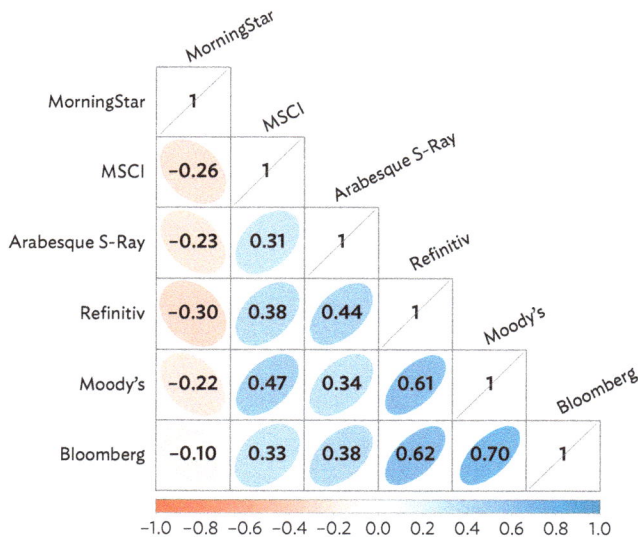

ESG = environmental, social, and governance; MSCI = Morgan Stanley Capital International.

Notes: In panel (a), rating items from MSCI, Refinitiv, Bloomberg, and S-Ray are considered in the analysis. This chart shows the number (percentage) of common items among raters. Panel (b) shows the correlations of ESG scores among different ESG raters, covering the sample in 2019. MorningStar scores evaluate ESG risk, which is negatively related to other ratings.

Sources: Panel (a) is based on Keeley, Alexander, Andrew Chapman, Kenichi Yoshida, Jun Xie, Janaki Imbulana, Shutaro Takeda, and Shunsuke Managi. 2022. "ESG Metrics and Social Equity: Investigating Commensurability." *Frontiers in Sustainability*. 3 (2022); Panel (b) is based on authors' calculations.

Figure 24: Environmental, Social, and Governance Ratings across Economies

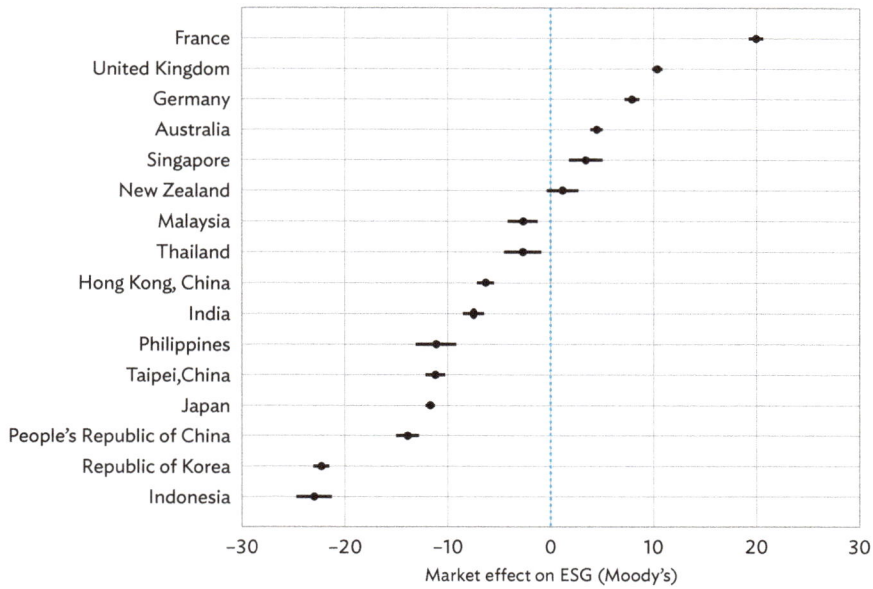

ESG = environmental, social, and governance.

Notes: The sample covers 13,927 firm-year observations from 38 economies during 2013–2022. The error bar denotes a 95% confidence interval.

Source: Authors' compilation based on Moody's Environmental, Social, and Governance Database.

Figure 25: Financial Impacts of Environmental, Social, and Governance Ratings across Economies

(a)

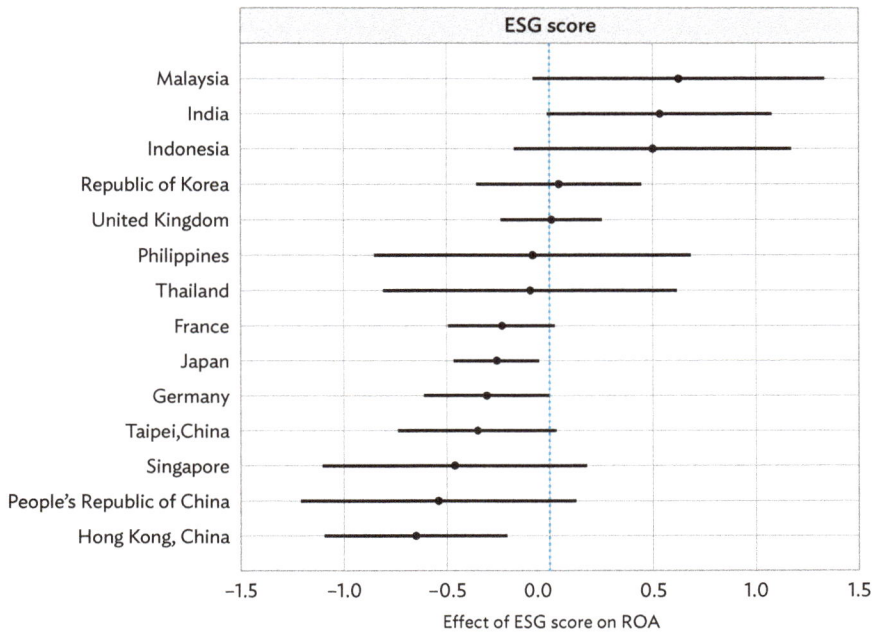

continued on next page

Figure 25   *continued*

(b)

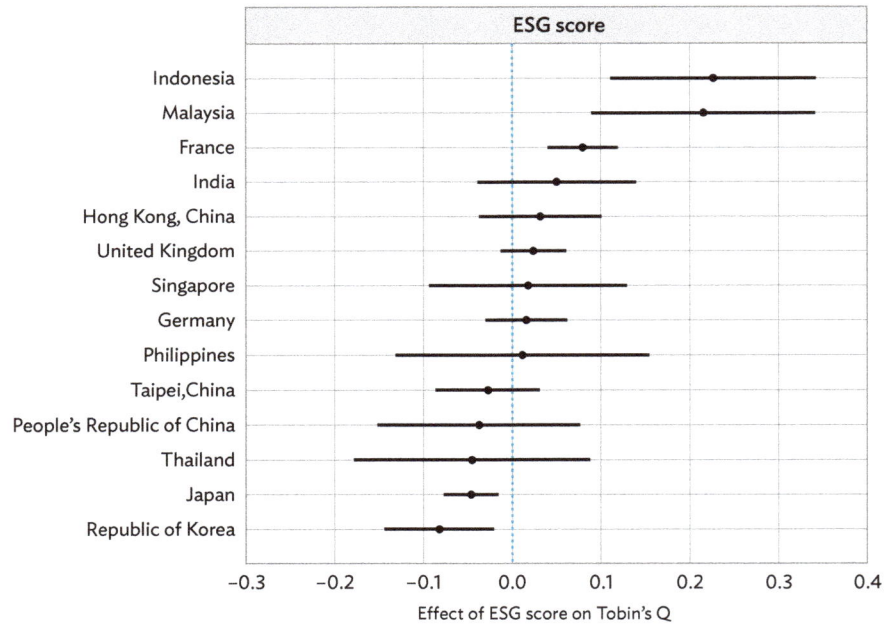

ESG score

Country	

Indonesia
Malaysia
France
India
Hong Kong, China
United Kingdom
Singapore
Germany
Philippines
Taipei,China
People's Republic of China
Thailand
Japan
Republic of Korea

Effect of ESG score on Tobin's Q

ESG = environmental, social, and governance; ROA = return on assets.

Notes: The analysis utilizes Moody's ESG rating as ESG performance. The sample covers 16,327 firm-year observations from 38 economies during 2013–2022. The error bar denotes a 95% confidence interval.

Sources: Authors' compilation based on Moody's Environmental, Social, and Governance Database and financial information from Refinitiv Eikon.

This study highlights the necessity of a standardized ESG assessment methodology to enable better comparability in making investment and business decisions. Transparency in the assessment process is crucial to enhancing the understanding of ESG ratings. Investors are encouraged to consider market-specific differences, while practitioners are advised to tailor ESG solutions to the company context and the domestic socioeconomic environment.

In conclusion, this study underscores the importance of nuanced considerations in ESG practices, accounting for methodological disparities and contextual factors. It recommends transparency, standardized methodologies, and the use of company- and market-specific contexts as key elements for businesses and investors navigating the complex landscape of ESG.

AsianBondsOnline Annual Bond Market Liquidity Survey

Introduction

AsianBondOnline conducts an annual local currency (LCY) bond market liquidity survey to gather information and insights from market participants on overall bond market developments and liquidity conditions in emerging East Asia.[6] This includes identifying various market-driven and macroeconomic factors that have contributed to the conditions in each bond market. The survey also includes an assessment of current market infrastructure and policies and regulations in place that may help relevant stakeholders in identifying areas for improvement to further develop and deepen LCY bond markets in the region.

The 2023 liquidity survey was conducted online in December 2023 among bond market participants in emerging East Asia. These included bond traders, brokers, fund managers, research houses, bond pricing agencies, and supervisory institutions. The survey was structured to assess both the quantitative and qualitative aspects of LCY government and corporate bond markets in the region. The quantitative section included metrics such as bid–ask spreads and transaction sizes. Meanwhile, the qualitative section includes a rating system on the level of development of each bond market in terms of market infrastructure and regulations. The survey also included a section on the respondents' interest and participation in the sustainable bond market, along with factors that affect the trading of sustainable bonds.

Overall Liquidity Conditions

The 2023 survey noted improved liquidity conditions in most LCY bond markets in the region compared to the previous year. Around 68.2% of respondents reported an increase in liquidity, compared to the corresponding number of 33.3% in 2022 (**Figure 26**). LCY bond markets experienced increased liquidity in 2023 due to relatively improved financial conditions, especially in the second half of year, with the United States (US) Federal Reserve signaling the end of its rate-hiking cycle. The possible

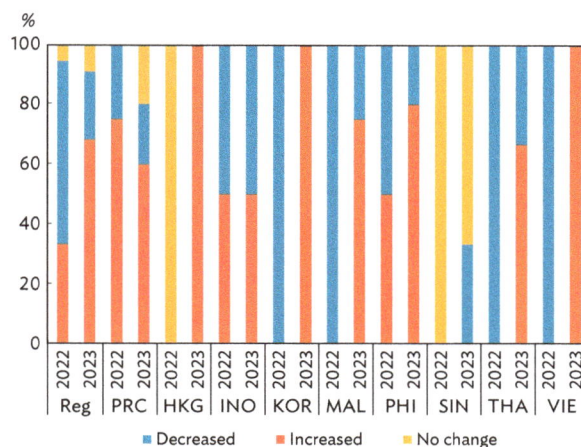

Figure 26: Liquidity Conditions by Economy in Emerging East Asia

HKG = Hong Kong, China; INO = Indonesia; KOR = Republic of Korea; MAL = Malaysia; PHI = Philippines; PRC = People's Republic of China; Reg = Regional; SIN = Singapore; THA = Thailand; VIE = Viet Nam.
Note: Figures refer to the share of survey respondents indicating either "no change," "decreased," or "increased."
Source: *AsianBondsOnline* 2023 Local Currency Bond Market Liquidity Survey.

ending of domestic monetary policy tightening across the region, and even easing in some markets, also contributed to increased trading activity. For example, central banks in the People's Republic of China (PRC) and Viet Nam cut their respective policy rates in 2023 (Table B in the *Developments in Regional Financial Conditions* section) to support economic growth.

Domestic monetary policy stances continued to be the most prominent factor that affected bond market liquidity in the region in 2023 (Figure 27). This was most evident in the PRC and Viet Nam, which had the region's highest shares of respondents citing domestic monetary policy as the top factor. The People's Bank of China and the State Bank of Vietnam both cut their respective policy rates in 2023 to support economic growth and stabilize weak property markets. Market sentiment was the second-most important domestic driver of bond market liquidity in emerging East Asia, as market participants

---

[6] Emerging East Asia is defined to include member states of the Association of Southeast Asian Nations (ASEAN) plus the People's Republic of China; Hong Kong, China; and the Republic of Korea.

Figure 27: Factors Affecting Bond Market Liquidity in Emerging East Asia in 2023

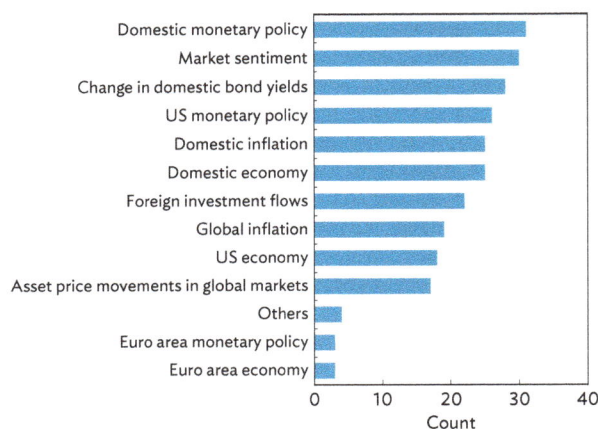

US = United States.
Source: *AsianBondsOnline* 2023 Local Currency Bond Market Liquidity Survey.

Figure 28: Average Bid–Ask Spreads for On-the-Run Government Bonds

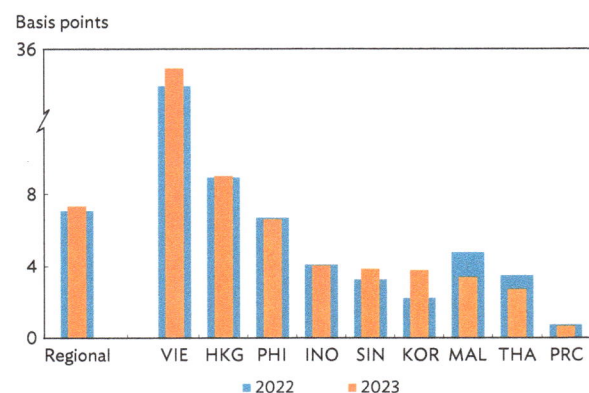

HKG = Hong Kong, China; INO = Indonesia; KOR = Republic of Korea; MAL = Malaysia; PHI = Philippines; PRC = People's Republic of China; SIN = Singapore; THA = Thailand; VIE = Viet Nam.
Note: The regional bid–ask spread refers to the average spread of the nine markets of emerging East Asia.
Source: *AsianBondsOnline* calculations based on Bloomberg LP data.

Figure 29: Average Bid–Ask Spreads for Off-the-Run Government Bonds

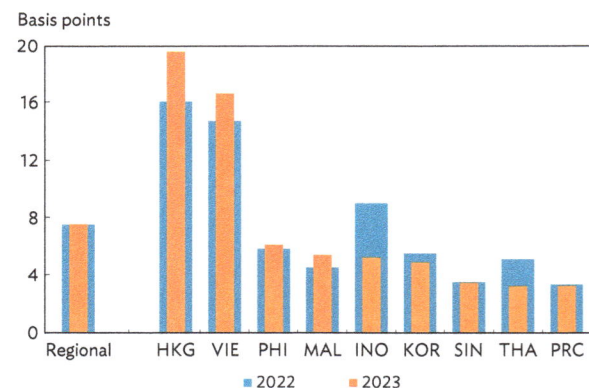

HKG = Hong Kong, China; INO = Indonesia; KOR = Republic of Korea; MAL = Malaysia; PHI = Philippines; PRC = People's Republic of China; SIN = Singapore; THA = Thailand; VIE = Viet Nam.
Note: The regional bid–ask spread refers to the average spread of the nine markets of emerging East Asia.
Source: *AsianBondsOnline* calculations based on Bloomberg LP data.

will time their trade based on expectations of changes in the monetary policy stances of domestic central banks and the Federal Reserve. US monetary policy is the most important global factor affecting bond market liquidity in the region.

Government Bond Markets

Liquidity

Government bond bid–ask spreads narrowed in most emerging East Asian economies amid improved financial conditions. Data compiled by *AsianBondsOnline* showed that the region's average bid–ask spread for on-the-run government bonds was largely unchanged at 7.4 basis points (bps) in 2023 from 7.1 bps in 2022 (**Figure 28**). Similarly, the region's average bid–ask spread for off-the-run government bonds in 2023 was unchanged from the previous year at 7.5 bps (**Figure 29**). Five out of nine markets in the region posted lower bid–ask spreads in 2023 than in the previous year. Across the region, Viet Nam had the largest government bid–ask-spread at 32.0 bps in 2023, up from 29.5 bps in the prior year on decreased issuance of government bonds. Notably, most member economies of the Association of Southeast Asian Nations posted narrower bid–ask spreads in 2023 than in 2022, reflecting improved liquidity amid strengthening financial conditions facilitated by stabilized inflation and the ending of monetary policy tightening in regional economies.

The typical transaction size for government bonds in the region rose slightly, indicating improved liquidity in most regional markets. The region's average transaction size for on-the-run government bonds slightly rose from USD3.6 million in 2022 to USD3.7 million in 2023 (**Figure 30**). Most of the region's markets showed either similar or larger transaction sizes for on-the-run

Figure 30: Typical Transaction Size for On-the-Run Government Bonds

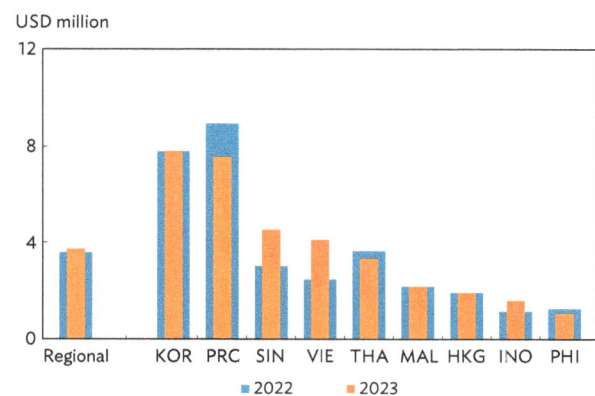

USD million

HKG = Hong Kong, China; INO = Indonesia; KOR = Republic of Korea; MAL = Malaysia; PHI = Philippines; PRC = People's Republic of China; SIN = Singapore; THA = Thailand; USD = United States dollar, VIE = Viet Nam.

Note: The regional transaction size refers to the average transaction size of the nine markets of emerging East Asia.

Source: *AsianBondsOnline* 2023 Local Currency Bond Market Liquidity Survey.

Figure 31: Local Currency Government Bond Market Structural Issues in Emerging East Asia

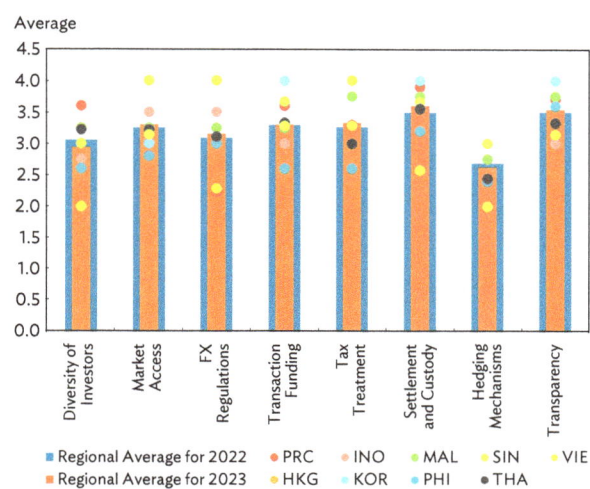

Average

Legend: Regional Average for 2022; Regional Average for 2023; PRC; HKG; INO; KOR; MAL; PHI; SIN; THA; VIE

FX = foreign exchange; HKG = Hong Kong, China; INO = Indonesia; KOR = Republic of Korea; MAL = Malaysia; PHI = Philippines; PRC = People's Republic of China; SIN = Singapore; THA = Thailand; VIE = Viet Nam.

Source: *AsianBondsOnline* 2023 Local Currency Bond Market Liquidity Survey.

government bonds in 2023 versus 2022. The average transaction size fell the most in the PRC, from USD8.9 million in 2022 to USD7.5 million in 2023, due in part to concerns about the weakened property market and its spillover to economic activities.

Market Development

Based on the responses of survey participants in 2023, the LCY government bond market in emerging East Asia showed a slight improvement in terms of structural factors (Figure 31). Among eight factors, the average score for the region was higher in six aspects compared with the results from the survey conducted in 2022.

Settlement and custody, along with transparency, were rated the highest among the eight structural issues in emerging East Asian government bond market. With an average score of 3.6, government bond markets in the region are perceived to have well-developed settlement and custody services. These allow investors to trade securely and efficiently. The regional mean score for transparency was 3.5, indicating good access to trading information such as auction results and pricing through reliable trading platforms.

Market access, transaction funding, foreign exchange regulations, and tax treatment of government bonds each received stable scores in 2023. For these four aspects, the regional average scores were 3.2–3.3, similar to their respective 2022 levels. Hong Kong, China and Singapore both achieved the highest score possible (4.0) for market access, foreign exchange regulations, and tax treatment as global financial centers. In both of these regional markets, government bonds can be widely traded by investors, with less exchange regulations and low taxes. On the other hand, the Philippines received a relatively low score of 2.6 in transaction funding and tax treatment, as its government bond market has limited diversity in terms of funding sources and relatively higher taxes compared with other emerging East Asian peers. The PRC and Viet Nam received relatively low scores of 2.2 to 2.3, respectively, on foreign exchange regulation.

The diversity of the investor base and hedging mechanisms in government bond markets need further development in emerging East Asia. The average scores of these two structural factors were relatively low compared to other indicators and both declined in 2023. The diversity of investors got an average score of 2.9, while hedging mechanism received an average score of 2.6—both of which were down from last year's levels of 3.1 and 2.7, respectively. Government bond markets in the region continued to be dominated by few market participants such as banks (Figure 5 in the *Bond Market Developments in the Fourth Quarter of 2023* section). There is also a lack of available hedging instruments to mitigate investment risks in most regional government bond markets.

Corporate Bond Markets

Liquidity

The majority of the participants in this year's liquidity survey noted an active secondary market for corporate bonds in 2023. Survey results indicated that 68% of participants observed an active secondary market for corporate bonds, a slight improvement from last year's response of 64% (**Figure 32**). However, 32% of survey respondents still considered there to be no active trading of corporate bonds in emerging East Asia. The region's corporate bond markets continue to lag government bond markets in terms of liquidity, as they tend to be dominated by buy-and-hold investors.

Similar to the government bond markets, liquidity in the region's corporate bond markets improved in 2023. The average bid–ask spread for the region's corporate bond market declined in 2023 (**Figure 33**). Among markets where data are available, the Philippines continued to register the highest bid–ask spread in the region, as its corporate bond market remained relatively

small and comprised only a few major issuers. While in five regional corporate bond markets, bid–ask spreads were stable or declined in 2023, bid–ask spread rose slightly in Indonesia and Hong Kong, China.

The average transaction size for emerging East Asia's corporate bond market marginally rose to USD3.7 million in 2023 from USD3.6 million in 2022. In most regional markets, survey participants noted either an increase or a similar transaction size to that of the previous year's survey (**Figure 34**). The only markets

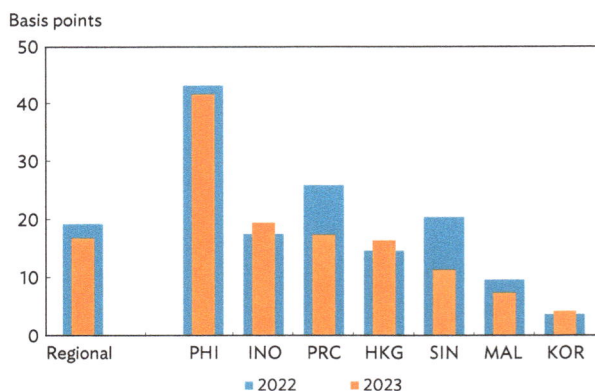

Figure 33: Average Bid–Ask Spreads for Corporate Bonds

HKG = Hong Kong, China; INO = Indonesia; KOR = Republic of Korea; MAL = Malaysia; PHI = Philippines; PRC = People's Republic of China; SIN = Singapore.
Note: The regional bid–ask spread refers to the average spread of the seven markets in emerging East Asia, where data are available.
Source: *AsianBondsOnline* calculations based on Bloomberg LP data.

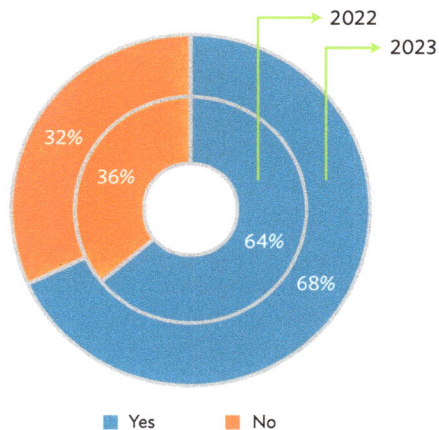

Figure 32: Is There an Active Secondary Bond Market for Corporate Bonds?

Note: Percentages refer to the share of survey respondents answering either "yes" or "no."
Source: *AsianBondsOnline* 2023 Local Currency Bond Market Liquidity Survey.

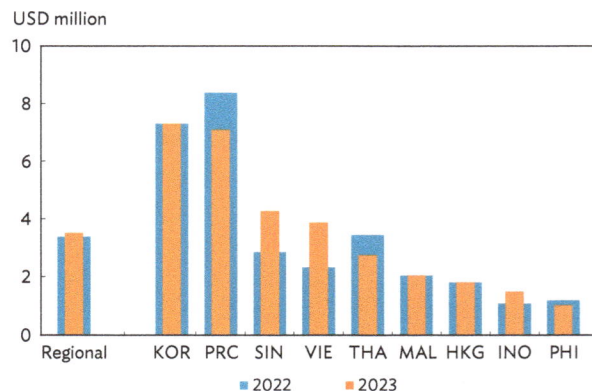

Figure 34: Average Transaction Sizes for Corporate Bonds

HKG = Hong Kong, China; INO = Indonesia; KOR = Republic of Korea; MAL = Malaysia; PHI = Philippines; PRC = People's Republic of China; SIN = Singapore; THA = Thailand; USD = United States dollar; VIE = Viet Nam.
Note: The regional transaction size refers to the average transaction size of the nine markets of emerging East Asia.
Source: *AsianBondsOnline* 2023 Local Currency Bond Market Liquidity Survey.

where the mean transaction size declined were in the PRC, Thailand, and the Philippines.

Market Development

The 2023 liquidity survey showed similar ratings for key structural factors in emerging East Asian corporate bond markets compared to 2022, and when compared to the region's government bond markets. The majority of the structural factors scored an average of 3.0 or above, while diversity of the investor profile and hedging mechanisms remained the areas that need further development in the region's corporate bond market (**Figure 35**). Among all key structural factors, similar to government bond markets, settlement and custody recorded the highest regional average score of 3.5, a marginal improvement from 3.2 in 2022. Foreign exchange regulations, tax treatment, and transparency all showed marginal improvements in 2023, having reported a slightly higher regional average rating of 3.2 each, while market access retained a regional average rating of 3.0. Similar to government bond markets, emerging East Asian corporate bond markets need to further diversify their investor profile and provide hedging tools for investors. Corporate bond markets in the region recorded a regional average score of 2.5 for diversity of investor profile, while hedging mechanisms scored 2.2. Almost all markets in emerging East Asia continued to

lack proper risk management tools needed by investors to effectively manage risks.

Sustainable Bond Markets

Similar to the 2022 survey, the liquidity survey included questions pertaining to the sustainable bond market. This section is meant to guide policymakers and regulators in further developing their sustainable bond markets. It is also intended to aid in the development of environmental, social, and governance (ESG) frameworks and promote sustainable investing in the region. Survey participants were asked about their interest in sustainable bond investments and requested to identify factors affecting sustainable bond investment interest.

Investors in emerging East Asia continued to exhibit a high level of interest in investing in sustainable bonds. In 2023, 76.2% of respondents said that they or their respective firm intend to trade and invest in sustainable bonds (**Figure 36**). While this represents a high percentage of respondents, it was lower than the previous year's 80%. Among the various factors, the firm's inclusion of ESG criteria as part of its overall objectives was rated as the most cited reason for interest in trading sustainable bonds (**Figure 37, Panel A**). This suggests that firms are increasingly recognizing the importance of ESG investing as a key part of its strategic objectives. Related to this, rising market interest was the second-most cited reason for interest in ESG investing. Among investors who either had no plans or do not invest in sustainable bonds,

Figure 35: Local Currency Corporate Bond Market Structural Issues in Emerging East Asia

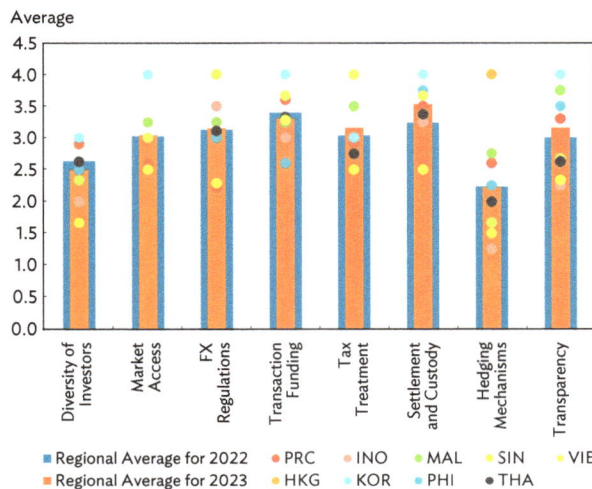

FX = foreign exchange; HKG = Hong Kong, China; INO = Indonesia; KOR = Republic of Korea; MAL = Malaysia; PHI = Philippines; PRC = People's Republic of China; SIN = Singapore; THA = Thailand; VIE = Viet Nam.
Source: *AsianBondsOnline* 2023 Local Currency Bond Market Liquidity Survey.

Figure 36: Interest in Trading Sustainable Bonds across Markets

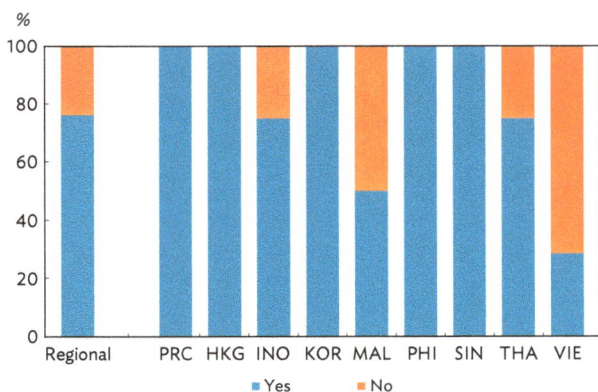

HKG = Hong Kong, China; INO = Indonesia; KOR = Republic of Korea; MAL = Malaysia; PHI = Philippines; PRC = People's Republic of China; SIN = Singapore; THA = Thailand; VIE = Viet Nam.
Source: *AsianBondsOnline* 2023 Local Currency Bond Market Liquidity Survey.

Figure 37: Factors Affecting Sustainable Bond Investment

Panel A. Participants who answered "Yes" to investing in ESG

Panel B. Participants who answered "No" to investing in ESG

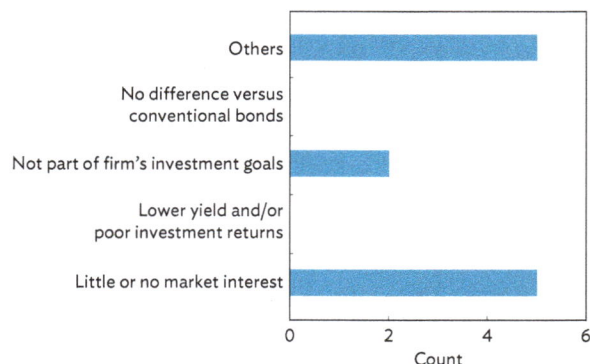

ESG = environmental, social, and governance.
Source: *AsianBondsOnline* 2023 Local Currency Bond Market Liquidity Survey.

responses were evenly split between lack of market interest and other factors (**Figure 37, Panel B**). Among other factors, a commonly cited reason that dampens interest in investing in ESG bonds is the relatively low liquidity of ESG bonds. The exclusion of ESG bonds as part of a firm's investment goals was also cited. In terms of the lack of liquidity and exclusion, governments and regulators can help to improve the depth of ESG bond markets and increase investor education on the merits of ESG investing.

When asked about liquidity, 40.6% of the participants said that sustainable bond market liquidity was roughly comparable to that of conventional bond markets. Another 40.6% noted that ESG bonds were less liquid than conventional bonds, which was higher than in the previous year's survey (**Figure 38**). While sustainable bond markets are relatively smaller than conventional bond markets, efforts should still be made to improve liquidity, as it was cited earlier in this discussion that liquidity is a factor in determining investments in ESG bond.

Figure 38: Sustainable Bond Market Liquidity

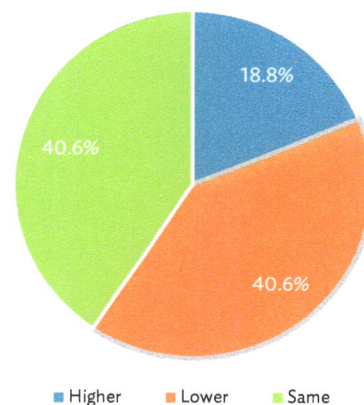

Source: *AsianBondsOnline* 2023 Local Currency Bond Market Liquidity Survey.

Market Summaries

People's Republic of China

Yield Movements

Local currency (LCY) government bond yields in the People's Republic of China (PRC) fell for all maturities between 1 December 2023 and 29 February 2024 due to expectations of monetary policy easing in the United States (US) and a slowdown in the domestic economy. The PRC's yields fell for all tenors by an average of 38 basis points (bps) on rising expectations that the US Federal Reserve would soon ease its monetary policy (**Figure 1**). Despite uncertainties over US monetary policy, yields continued to fall in January and February as the People's Bank of China eased monetary policy to help lower funding costs and support the economy. On 24 January, the People's Bank of China reduced the reserve requirement ratio of financial institutions by 50 bps. This was followed by a 25 bps reduction in the 5-year loan prime rate to 3.95% on 20 February. Yields were also depressed due to the persistence of deflation in the PRC, which dipped further to −0.8% year-on-year in January from −0.3% year-on-year in December.

Figure 1: The People's Republic of China's Benchmark Yield Curve—Local Currency Government Bonds

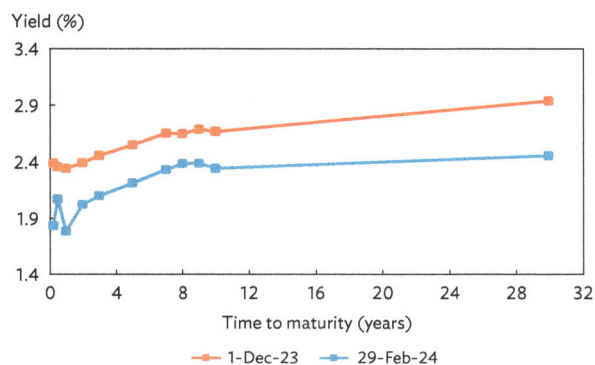

Source: Based on data from Bloomberg LP.

Local Currency Bond Market Size and Issuance

The PRC's LCY bonds outstanding grew at an accelerated pace in the fourth quarter (Q4) of 2023 as the government sought to support the domestic economy. Total LCY bonds outstanding grew 2.7% quarter-on-quarter (q-o-q) in Q4 2023 to CNY142.7 trillion, up from 2.5% q-o-q in the third quarter (**Figure 2**). Despite a contraction in issuance during the quarter, outstanding government bonds rose 4.5% q-o-q, compared with 3.2% q-o-q in the third quarter of 2023, due to reduced maturities. In contrast, corporate bonds outstanding declined 0.4% q-o-q in Q4 2023 over weakened economic conditions.

Figure 2: Composition of Local Currency Bonds Outstanding in the People's Republic of China

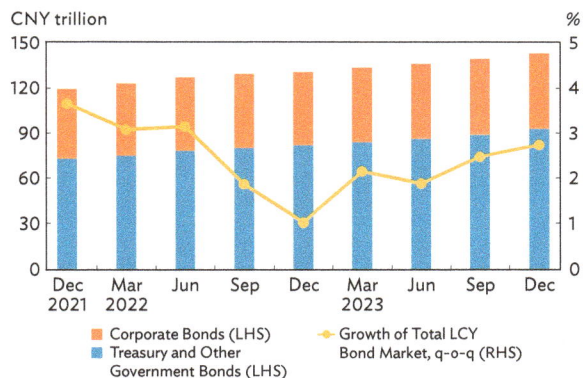

CNY = Chinese yuan, LCY = local currency, LHS = left-hand side, q-o-q = quarter-on-quarter, RHS = right-hand side.
Source: CEIC Data Company.

This market summary was written by Russ Jason Lo, consultant, Economic Research and Development Impact Department, ADB, Manila.

The PRC's LCY bond sales totaled CNY11.2 trillion in Q4 2023, a 7.9% q-o-q decline from the previous quarter on reduced sales from both government and corporate issuers (**Figure 3**). Government issuance declined 3.8% q-o-q in Q4 2023 largely due to a decline in local government bond issuance, which fell 16.2% q-o-q, and policy bank bonds, which fell 38.5% q-o-q. The decline in local government bonds was due to local governments having completed 2023 bond quotas at the end of September, although there was also some frontloading of 2024 issuance quotas in Q4 2023. Treasury bond issuance increased 18.0% q-o-q on increased fiscal spending. Heightened investor concerns over economic conditions and the property market led to a drop in corporate bond issuance of 13.4% q-o-q.

Investor Profile

Commercial banks remained the largest holder of the PRC's LCY government bonds at the end of December 2023 (**Figure 4**). Commercial banks are the largest investor in the PRC's government bond market. Commercial banks had an overall share of 79.1% at the end of December and were also the dominant holder for all different government bond types, including an 85.1% share of local government bonds outstanding.

Figure 3: Composition of Local Currency Bond Issuance in the People's Republic of China

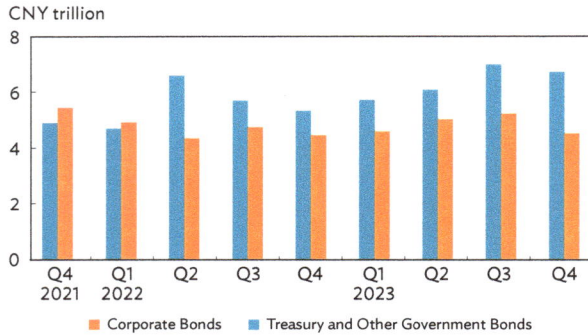

CNY = Chinese yuan, Q1 = first quarter, Q2 = second quarter, Q3 = third quarter, Q4 = fourth quarter.
Source: CEIC Data Company.

Figure 4: Investor Profile of Government Bonds

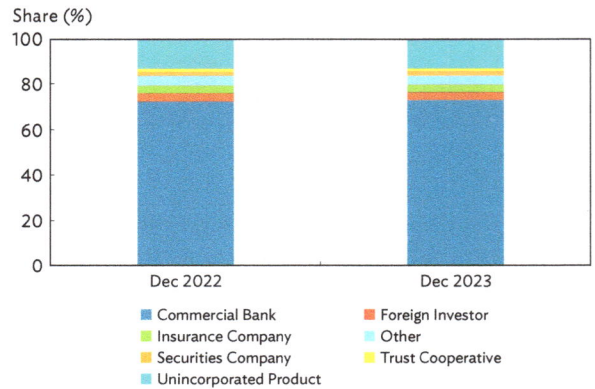

Note: Government bonds include bonds issued by local governments, policy banks, and the central government.
Source: CEIC Data Company.

Hong Kong, China

Yield Movements

Local currency (LCY) government bond yields in Hong Kong, China fell for most tenors between 1 December 2023 and 29 February 2024, driven primarily by expectations that the Federal Reserve would cut its policy rate during the second half of the year (**Figure 1**). Bond yields declined by an average of 58 basis points for bonds with short-term maturities but rose an average of 10 basis points for 10-year to 20-year tenors as the longer-term yields tracked US yields. Moderating inflation also contributed to the decline in bond yields. Hong Kong, China's consumer price inflation eased further to 1.7% year-on-year (y-o-y) in January from 2.4% y-o-y in December and 2.6% y-o-y in November.

Local Currency Bond Market Size and Issuance

LCY bonds outstanding in Hong Kong, China saw modest growth of 0.3% quarter-on-quarter (q-o-q) in the fourth quarter (Q4) of 2023, reaching a size of HKD3.0 trillion at the end of December (**Figure 2**). Growth in the LCY bond market in Q4 2023 was driven primarily by an expansion in outstanding Exchange Fund Bills and Notes, while both Hong Kong Special Administrative Region (HKSAR) bonds and corporate bonds posted q-o-q contractions due to weaker issuance. Corporate bonds (HKD1.5 trillion) comprised 49.1% of Hong Kong, China's total LCY bond market at the end of December. Exchange Fund Bills and Notes (HKD1.3 trillion) and HKSAR bonds (HKD0.3 trillion) accounted for the remaining 41.5% and 9.4% shares, respectively.

Figure 1: Hong Kong, China's Benchmark Yield Curve— Local Currency Government Bonds

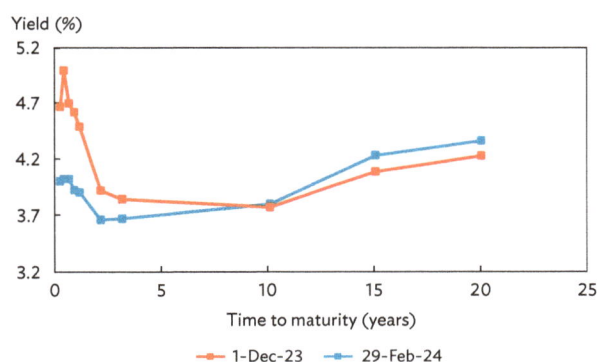

Source: Based on data from Bloomberg LP.

Figure 2: Composition of Local Currency Bonds Outstanding in Hong Kong, China

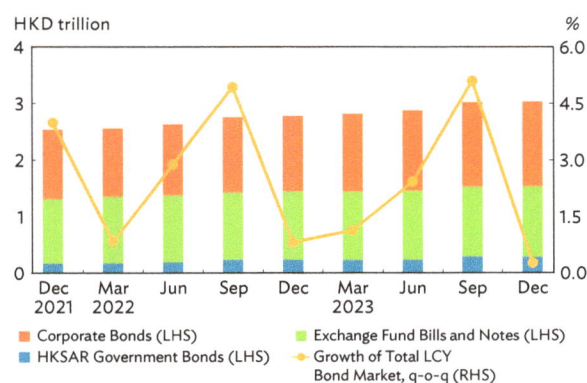

HKD = Hong Kong dollar, HKSAR = Hong Kong Special Administrative Region, LCY = local currency, LHS = left-hand side, q-o-q = quarter-on-quarter, RHS = right-hand side.
Source: Hong Kong Monetary Authority.

This market summary was written by Debbie Gundaya, consultant, Economic Research and Development Impact Department, ADB, Manila.

LCY debt sales in Hong Kong, China fell 6.3% q-o-q to HKD1.2 trillion in Q4 2023 due to weaker issuance of HKSAR and corporate bonds (Figure 3). HKSAR bond issuance totaled HKD30.5 billion, including HKD20.0 billion of retail green bonds issued in October.[7] Nonetheless, HKSAR bond sales fell 47.9% q-o-q in Q4 2023, as there was a relatively large volume of Silver Bond issuance in the prior quarter.[8] Corporate bond issuance tallied HKD192.8 billion in Q4 2023, contracting 26.8% q-o-q as interest rates remained elevated and uncertainties lingered regarding the impact of slowing global growth on the domestic economy. Meanwhile, the issuance of Exchange Fund Bills and Exchange Fund Notes posted a modest increase of 1.6% q-o-q, totaling HKD1.0 trillion in Q4 2023.

Figure 3: Composition of Local Currency Bond Issuance in Hong Kong, China

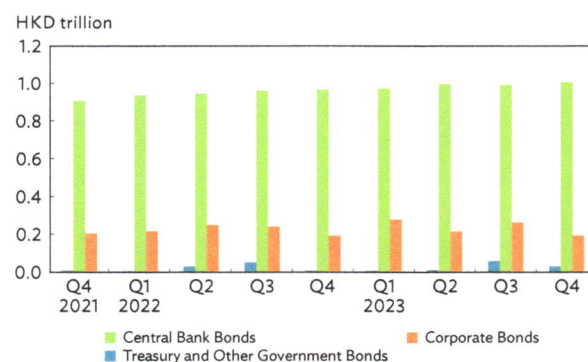

HKD = Hong Kong dollar, Q1 = first quarter, Q2 = second quarter, Q3 = third quarter, Q4 = fourth quarter.
Source: Hong Kong Monetary Authority.

---

[7] This was the second batch of retail green bonds issued by the Government of the Hong Kong Special Administrative Region of the People's Republic of China following an inaugural issuance worth HKD20.0 billion in May 2022. Proceeds of the 3-year bonds go to Hong Kong, China's Capital Works Reserve Fund to finance public works projects with environmental benefits.
[8] Silver Bonds are 3-year inflation-linked government bonds restricted for purchase by citizens aged 60 years and older.

Indonesia

Yield Movements

Between 1 December 2023 and 29 February 2024, local currency (LCY) government bond yields in Indonesia edged down for all maturities (Figure 1). Bond yields declined an average of 18 basis points across the curve amid signals that the United States Federal Reserve would cut rates later this year. While the timing of the Federal Reserve rate cut remained uncertain, subdued inflation contributed to the overall decline in bond yields during the review period. This has led Bank Indonesia to keep its policy rate unchanged at 6.00% since October 2023. However, at its 20–21 February meeting, Bank Indonesia Governor Perry Warjiyo noted that a rate cut is likely in the second half of the year.

Local Currency Bond Market Size and Issuance

Indonesia's LCY bond market growth picked up in the fourth quarter (Q4) of 2023, with bonds outstanding reaching a size of IDR6,331.0 trillion at the end of December. Despite a contraction in the issuance of government and corporate bonds, overall growth climbed to 2.7% quarter-on-quarter (q-o-q) in Q4 2023 from 0.5% q-o-q in the third quarter (Q3), due to a low volume of maturities in Q4 2023 (**Figure 2**). Government bonds outstanding, which account for a 91.7% share of Indonesia's total LCY bond market, recorded a 2.6% q-o-q hike, up from only 0.5% q-o-q growth in Q3 2023. Corporate bonds expanded 3.5% q-o-q, reversing the marginal 0.02% q-o-q contraction in Q3 2023.

Figure 1: Indonesia's Benchmark Yield Curve—Local Currency Government Bonds

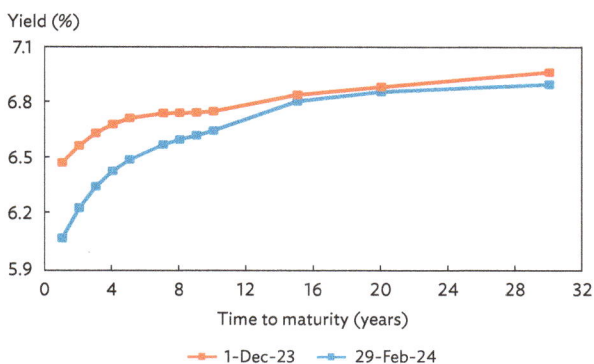

Source: Based on data from Bloomberg LP.

Figure 2: Composition of Local Currency Bonds Outstanding in Indonesia

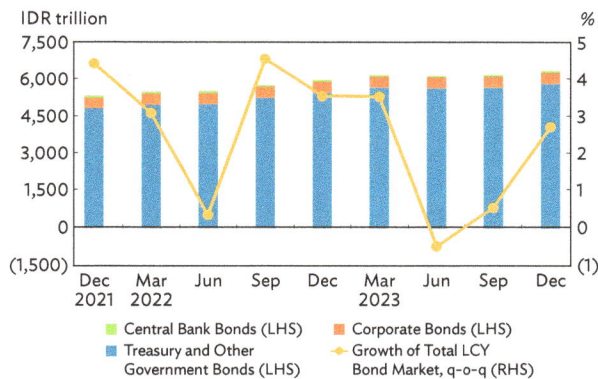

( ) = negative, IDR = Indonesian rupiah, LCY = local currency, LHS = left-hand side, q-o-q = quarter-on-quarter, RHS = right-hand side.
Note: Data include *sukuk* (Islamic bonds). Data for Treasury and other government bonds comprise tradable and nontradable central government bonds.
Sources: Bank Indonesia; Directorate General of Budget Financing and Risk Management, Ministry of Finance; and Indonesia Stock Exchange.

This market summary was written by Roselyn Regalado, consultant, Economic Research and Development Impact Department, ADB, Manila.

LCY bond issuance in Indonesia totaled IDR459.1 trillion in Q4 2023 on growth of 13.1% q-o-q that was largely driven by central bank issuance (Figure 3). Overall issuance growth in Q4 2023 was dragged down by declines in the issuance of government bonds and corporate bonds. Issuance of government bonds contracted as the government had mostly fulfilled its annual borrowing requirements in prior quarters. While corporate bond issuance was still substantial in Q4 2023, it was down 13.5% q-o-q following a high volume of issuance in Q3 2023 when the Federal Reserve halted its rate-hiking cycle. Among the largest corporate bond issuers during the quarter were Bank Rakyat Indonesia, OKI Pulp & Paper Mills, and Sarana Multigriya Finansial, representing 16.1%, 14.8%, and 7.4% of the Q4 2023 issuance total, respectively.

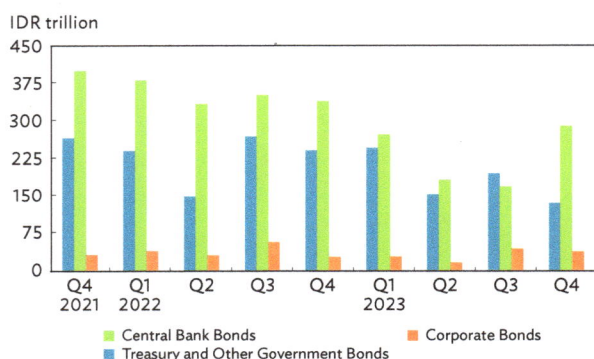

Figure 3: Composition of Local Currency Bond Issuance in Indonesia

IDR = Indonesian rupiah, Q1 = first quarter, Q2 = second quarter, Q3 = third quarter, Q4 = fourth quarter.
Note: Data include *sukuk* (Islamic bonds). Data for Treasury and other government bonds comprise tradable and nontradable central government bonds.
Sources: Bank Indonesia; Directorate General of Budget Financing and Risk Management, Ministry of Finance; and Indonesia Stock Exchange.

Investor Profile

At the end of December 2023, domestic investors still dominated holdings of both conventional and Islamic tradable government bonds in Indonesia. However, the shareholdings of domestic investors in Islamic bonds (98.4%) remained higher compared with conventional bonds (82.0%). Collectively, domestic investors held an 85.1% share of tradable government bonds in Indonesia at the end of December 2023, slightly down from their 85.6% share a year earlier. While banks remained the largest holder of government bonds, their holdings share slipped to 26.5% from 32.0% in the previous year (**Figure 4**). The second-largest domestic investor group was the central bank with a 19.4% share, the highest among its regional peers. Meanwhile, foreign investors increased their holdings share of Indonesian government bonds to 14.9% at the end of December 2023 from 14.4% at the end of December 2022 on positive sentiment over expectations the Federal Reserve would begin easing its policy rate in 2024. Nonetheless, Indonesia continued to be the region's most diverse market in terms of investor holdings, as it scored the lowest in emerging East Asia in terms of the Herfindahl–Hirschman Index.[9]

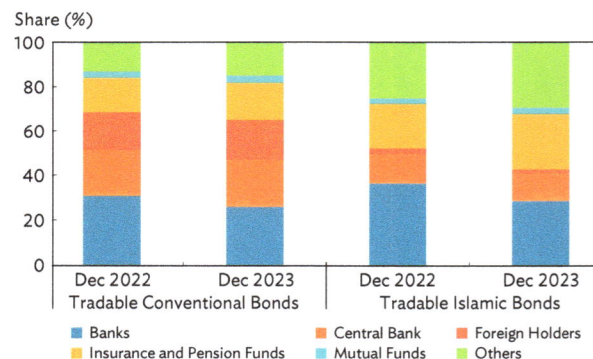

Figure 4: Investor Profile of Tradable Central Government Bonds

Source: Directorate General of Budget Financing and Risk Management, Ministry of Finance.

[9] The Herfindahl–Hirschman Index is a common measure of market concentration. The index is used to measure the investor profile diversification of the local currency bond market by summing the squared share of each investor group in the bond market.

Republic of Korea

Yield Movements

Local currency (LCY) government bond yields in the Republic of Korea fell for almost all tenors between 1 December 2023 and 29 February 2024 (Figure 1). Bond yields largely fell in December following the Federal Reserve meeting at which it lowered its quarterly median federal funds rate projections for 2024, boosting expectations that it will start easing this year. However, yields picked up again in January as the timing of the Federal Reserve's rate cuts remained uncertain. The decline in yields was also limited by the Bank of Korea's decision at its 11 January and 22 February monetary policy meetings to maintain its current restrictive monetary policy stance, lowering expectations of an early rate cut. The central bank deemed that even as inflation continued to slow, uncertainties regarding the inflation outlook remained. These include movements of global oil and agricultural product prices and the direction of domestic and global economic growth.

Local Currency Bond Market Size and Issuance

The Republic of Korea's total LCY bonds outstanding grew 1.6% quarter-on-quarter (q-o-q) to reach KRW3,217.0 trillion at the end of the fourth quarter (Q4) of 2023, led by an expansion in the corporate bond segment. Overall growth in the LCY bond market in Q4 2023 moderated from 2.4% q-o-q in the previous quarter as the stocks of government bonds and central bank bonds fell (**Figure 2**). Corporate bonds grew 3.1% q-o-q and continued to account for over half of the total LCY bond market in Q4 2023 due to a surge in issuance during the quarter. Meanwhile, government bonds outstanding declined 0.3% q-o-q due to reduced issuance during the quarter.

Figure 1: The Republic of Korea's Benchmark Yield Curve—Local Currency Government Bonds

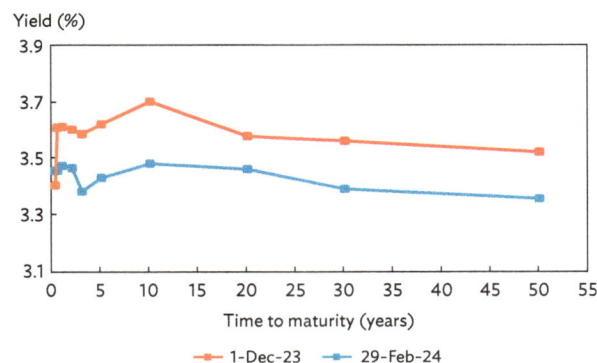

Source: Based on data from Bloomberg LP.

Figure 2: Composition of Local Currency Bonds Outstanding in the Republic of Korea

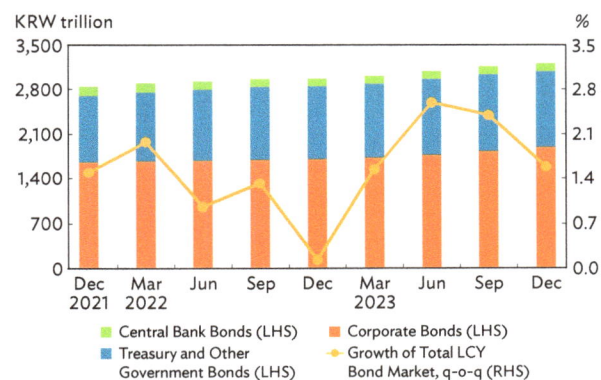

KRW = Korean won, LCY = local currency, LHS = left-hand side, q-o-q = quarter-on-quarter, RHS = right-hand side.
Sources: Bank of Korea and KG Zeroin Corp.

This market summary was written by Angelica Andrea Cruz, consultant, Economic Research and Development Impact Department, ADB, Manila.

Total LCY bond issuance rose 2.9% q-o-q to KRW298.7 trillion in Q4 2023, driven solely by the rebound in the corporate bond segment. Corporate bond issuance in the Republic of Korea surged 21.4% q-o-q in Q4 2023, a reversal from the 3.8% q-o-q decline in the third quarter (Q3) (**Figure 3**). Issuance rose during the quarter as companies refinanced maturing debt. Meanwhile, issuance of government bonds continued to fall in Q4 2023, declining 33.8% q-o-q, following a 12.9% q-o-q contraction in Q3 2023. This was the result of the government's frontloading policy of releasing 65% of the budget in the first half of the year and fulfilling most of its borrowing requirements by the end of Q3 2023.

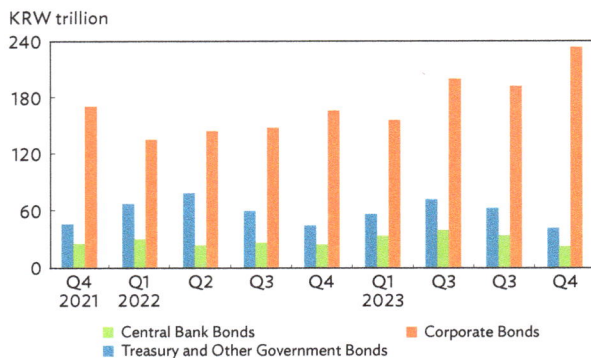

Figure 3: Composition of Local Currency Bond Issuance in the Republic of Korea

KRW = Korean won, Q1 = first quarter, Q2 = second quarter, Q3 = third quarter, Q4 = fourth quarter.
Sources: Bank of Korea and KG Zeroin Corp.

Investor Profile

Insurance companies and pension funds continued to hold the largest share of the Republic of Korea's LCY bonds outstanding. Insurance companies and pension funds held 27.8% of LCY government bonds outstanding at the end of September 2023, which was lower than their 31.2% share a year earlier. Banks and foreign investors were also among the top investor groups in the LCY government bond market with holdings shares of 21.6% and 20.3%, respectively, at the end of September 2023 (**Figure 4**). Meanwhile, other financial institutions held 45.0% of all LCY corporate bonds outstanding, up from a 43.1% share in September 2022. Insurance companies and pension funds were the second-largest investor group with a holdings share of 28.6%, which was a notable decline from 32.6% a year earlier. Foreign holdings in the LCY corporate bond market remained negligible at the end of September 2023.

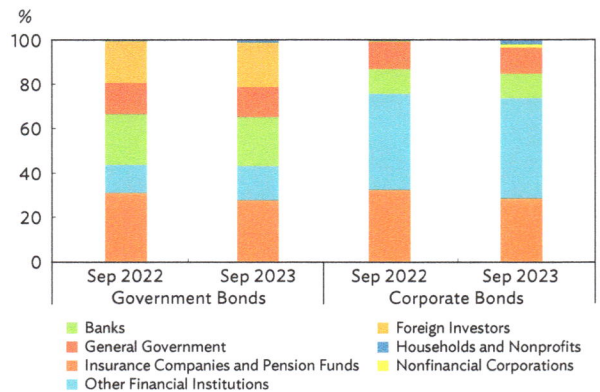

Figure 4: Local Currency Bonds Outstanding Investor Profile

Sources: *AsianBondsOnline* and Bank of Korea.

Lao People's Democratic Republic

Size and Composition

The Lao People's Democratic Republic's (PDR) bond market has grown significantly in the past decade, reaching a size of USD4.2 billion at the end of December 2022, up from USD0.1 billion in 2013, based on available data. In terms of relative size, the Lao PDR's bond market was equivalent to 34.0% of its gross domestic product (GDP) at the end of December 2022, slightly higher than that of Viet Nam (27.3%) (**Figure 1**). After the coronavirus disease (COVID-19) pandemic, the Lao PDR's local currency (LCY) bond market witnessed rapid expansion, with LCY bonds' share of the total bond market increasing from 10.0% in 2018 to 36.3% in 2022 (**Figure 2**).[10] In the same period, the ratio of share of foreign currency (FCY) bonds outstanding to GDP increased relatively less.

The Government of the Lao PDR has been able to raise both LCY and FCY financing from the domestic capital market. The government has been able to issue bonds through the Lao Securities Exchange in both

Lao kip and United States dollars to support cashflow management and strengthen debt management (**Figure 3**).

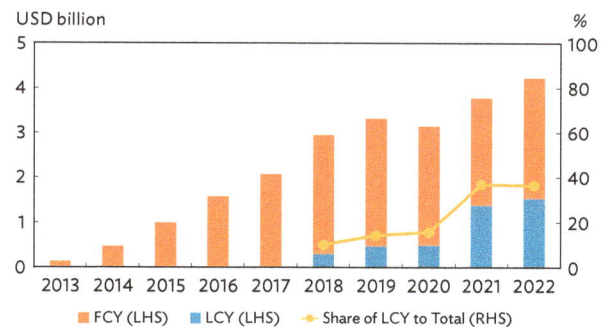

Figure 2: Composition of Total Bonds Outstanding in the Lao People's Democratic Republic

FCY = foreign-currency denominated, LCY = local-currency denominated, LHS = left-hand side, RHS = right-hand side, USD = United States dollar.
Notes:
1. FCY data include bonds issued in the Lao Securities Exchange, Singapore Exchange, and the Thai Bond Market Association.
2. Figures were computed based on 31 December 2022 currency exchange rates to remove currency effects.
Sources: Lao Securities Exchange, Ministry of Finance Lao PDR, Singapore Exchange, and Thai Bond Market Association.

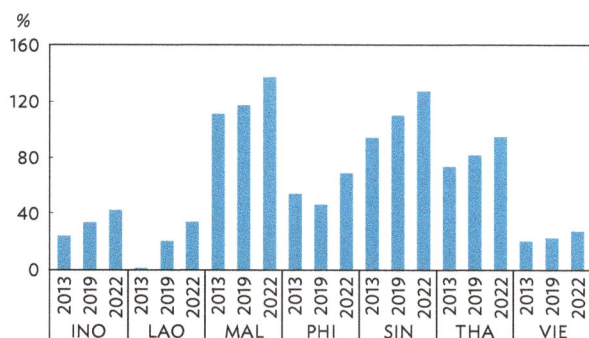

Figure 1: Bond Market as Share of GDP in ASEAN Economies

ASEAN = Association of Southeast Asian Nations, GDP = gross domestic product, INO = Indonesia, LAO = Lao People's Democratic Republic, MAL = Malaysia, PHI = Philippines, SIN = Singapore, THA = Thailand, VIE = Viet Nam.
Note: Data for GDP is from CEIC Data Company.
Source: AsiaBondsOnline calculations based on various sources.

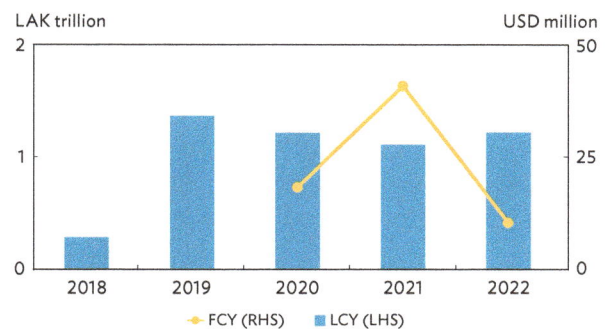

Figure 3: Government Bonds Issued through the Lao Securities Exchange

FCY = foreign currency, LAK = Lao kip, LCY = local currency, LHS = left-hand side, RHS = right-hand side, USD = United States dollar.
Source: Ministry of Finance Lao People's Democratic Republic.

This market summary was written by Emma Allen of the Lao PDR Resident Mission, ADB, Ventianne; and Angelica Andrea Cruz, consultant, Economic Research and Development Impact Department, ADB, Manila.

[10] Local currency bonds are bonds denominated in Lao kip, while foreign currency bonds are denominated in currencies other than the Lao kip. Definitions do not take into account where the bonds were issued (onshore or offshore).

Local Currency Bond Market Size and Issuance

The Lao PDR's LCY government bond market has grown since 2018, driven by LCY bond financing to support fiscal needs. Total LCY government bonds outstanding reached LAK26.6 trillion at the end of 2022, up from LAK24.0 trillion in 2021, due to the issuance of investment bonds and triangular bonds to finance domestic public investment (**Figure 4**).[11] By the end of 2022, investment bonds accounted for 56.9% (LAK15.1 trillion) of total LCY bonds outstanding, followed by triangular bonds (24.6%, LAK6.5 trillion). Treasury bills issued via the Lao Securities Exchange and the Bank of the Lao PDR collectively accounted for 18.5% (LAK4.9 trillion).

Foreign Currency Bond Market Size and Issuance

FCY bonds outstanding issued by the Government of the Lao PDR and the corporate sector grew from USD0.1 billion in 2013 to USD2.7 billion by the end of December 2022. This left the Lao PDR with the second-highest FCY-bonds-to-GDP share in ASEAN at 21.6% (**Figure 5**). Central government bonds used to dominate the Lao PDR's FCY bond market until 2018, with their share of the total declining from 56.3% in 2018 to 42.2% by the end of December 2022 as corporate bond issuances increased. In particular, hydropower companies—such as EDL Generation, Xayaburi Power, and Nam Ngum 2 Power—tapped the Thai bond market for financing. Thai baht (THB)-denominated bonds comprised 78.3% and 79.9% of the outstanding FCY government and corporate bonds, respectively, at the end of December 2022 (**Figure 6**). Meanwhile, USD-denominated bonds accounted for 21.7% of government bonds and 20.1% of corporate bonds outstanding during the same period.

The average maturity of outstanding FCY government bonds in the Lao PDR has been declining since 2017. At the end of December 2022, 38.8% of total FCY bonds outstanding had remaining tenors of more than 1 year to 3 years, 31.6% had tenors of more than 3 years to 5 years, and 27.7% had a tenor of more than 5 years to 10 years.

Figure 4: Composition of Local Currency Bonds Outstanding in the Lao People's Democratic Republic

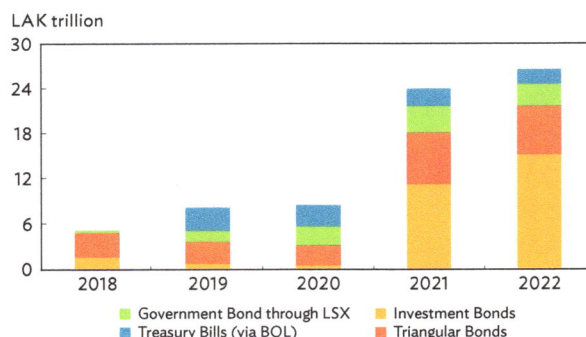

LAK trillion

Legend:
- Government Bond through LSX
- Investment Bonds
- Treasury Bills (via BOL)
- Triangular Bonds

BOL = Bank of the Lao People's Democratic Republic, LAK = Lao kip, LSX = Lao Securities Exchange.
Note: There are no available data for local currency corporate bonds.
Source: Ministry of Finance Lao People's Democratic Republic.

Figure 5: Foreign Currency Bonds Outstanding as Share of GDP in ASEAN, December 2022

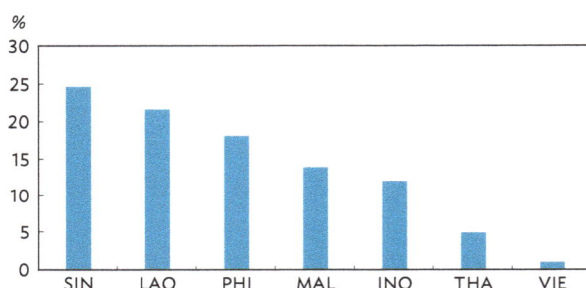

%

ASEAN = Association of Southeast Asian Nations, GDP = gross domestic product, INO = Indonesia, LAO = Lao People's Democratic Republic, MAL = Malaysia, PHI = Philippines, SIN = Singapore, THA = Thailand, VIE = Viet Nam.
Note: Data for GDP are from CEIC Data Company.
Source: *AsiaBondsOnline* calculations based on various sources.

(**Figure 7**). The average size-weighted tenor of FCY bonds outstanding in the Lao PDR declined from 6.8 years in 2017 to 4.0 years at the end of 2022. The shortened maturity profile will have implications for refinancing needs over the next few years.

The issuance of FCY bonds and their average tenor have both declined in recent years. During the pandemic, tightened liquidity conditions in international markets and weaker economic growth, both locally and

---

[11] Ministry of Finance of the Lao PDR. 2023. *Public and Publicly Guaranteed Debt Statistic Bulletin: 2022—Volume 4.* Vientiane.

Figure 6: Composition of Foreign Currency Bonds Outstanding by the Lao People's Democratic Republic

THB = Thai baht, USD = United States dollar.

Note: Figures were computed based on 31 December 2022 exchange rates to remove currency effects.

Sources: Lao Securities Exchange, Singapore Exchange, and Thai Bond Market Association.

Figure 8: Composition of Foreign Currency Bond Issuance in the Lao People's Democratic Republic's Bond Market

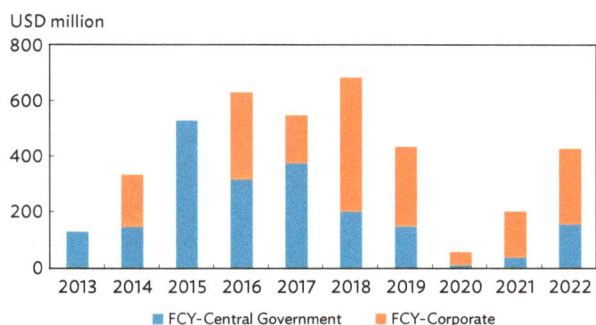

FCY = foreign currency, USD = United States dollar.

Note: Figures were computed based on 31 December 2022 currency exchange rates to remove currency effects.

Sources: Lao Securities Exchange, Singapore Exchange, and Thai Bond Market Association.

Figure 7: Maturity Structure of Foreign Currency Bonds Outstanding Issued in the Lao People's Democratic Republic's Bond Market

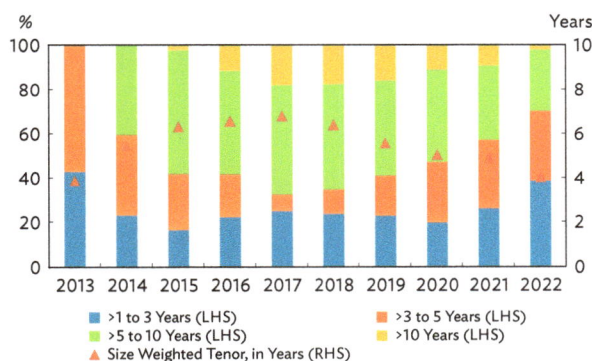

LHS = left-hand side, RHS = right-hand side.

Note: Figures were computed based on 31 December 2022 currency exchange rates to remove currency effects.

Sources: Lao Securities Exchange, Singapore Exchange, and Thai Bond Market Association.

Figure 9: Maturity Structure of Foreign Currency Bonds Issued by the Lao Securities Exchange

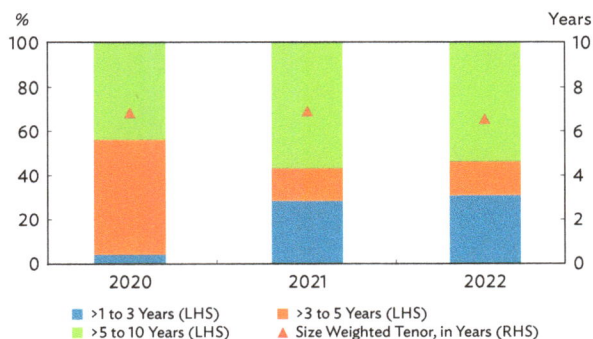

LHS = left-hand side, RHS = right-hand side.

Note: All bonds were issued in United States dollar.

Source: Lao Securities Exchange.

abroad, constrained the ability of Lao PDR issuers to tap FCY financing. The government has also reduced its external borrowing to improve its debt sustainability and fiscal position (**Figure 8**). Since then, the Lao PDR's total FCY government bond issuance volume has fallen. FCY bonds in United States dollars have been issued onshore by the Lao Securities Exchange since 2020. Tenors of these bonds ranged from 1 to 10 years and their coupon rates ranged from 5.0% to 8.0%. The average

size-weighted tenor of these bonds was 6.9 years in 2020, 7.0 years in 2021, and 6.6 years in 2022 (**Figure 9**).

Recent Developments

The Government of the Lao PDR is taking steps to further develop its domestic bond market, including issuance of bonds in a broader range of currencies, developing the corporate bond market, and expanding the investor base. In June 2023, the Souvanny Home Center, a distributor of construction materials and home products, became the first corporate issuer to sell USD3.0 million, equivalent to LAK57.2 billion, of USD-denominated bonds via the Lao Securities Exchange. In September 2023, the Government of the Lao PDR expanded the currencies of bond offerings in the domestic market and successfully sold its first bond denominated in Thai baht, worth THB3.0 billion, in its home market. The full subscription of these offerings is a reflection of investors' confidence in onshore issuance of both foreign and local currency bonds in the Lao PDR.

The Lao PDR's domestic bond market represents an important source of alternative funding for both the public and private sectors. It is therefore important to continue to invest in its medium- to long-term development. In the future, the Government of the Lao PDR plans to continue with domestic bond market development, including development of the secondary bond market, enhancing transparency and governance, and piloting use of auction mechanisms and signaling tools to strengthen communication with market participants for supporting cashflow management and enhancing debt management.

Malaysia

Yield Movements

Between 1 December 2023 and 29 February 2024, movements in the local currency (LCY) government bond yields of Malaysia were mixed as the timing of monetary policy easing by the United States Federal Reserve remained uncertain (Figure 1). Yields for most tenors declined an average of 4 basis points while those that increased jumped an average of 2 basis points. On 24 January, Bank Negara Malaysia decided to keep the overnight policy rate unchanged at 3.00%.

Figure 1: Malaysia's Benchmark Yield Curve—Local Currency Government Bonds

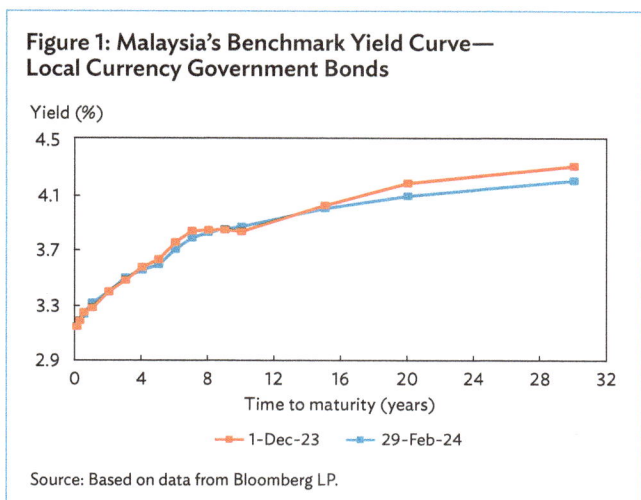

Source: Based on data from Bloomberg LP.

Local Currency Bond Market Size and Issuance

The LCY bond market of Malaysia grew in the fourth quarter (Q4) of 2023 as all bond segments recorded quarter-on-quarter (q-o-q) expansions. Outstanding LCY bonds increased 1.2% q-o-q to a value of MYR2.0 trillion at the end of 2023 (**Figure 2**). Bank Negara Malaysia bills led the growth among all LCY bond types, jumping 11.0% q-o-q as few of these securities matured during the review period. LCY corporate bonds outstanding also showed an uptick of 0.8% q-o-q due to increased issuance during the quarter. By the end of 2023, Malaysia's LCY bonds outstanding comprised 63.8% *sukuk*, with central bank and corporate *sukuk* leading the growth of the Islamic bond market. Growth in LCY *sukuk* marginally increased 0.4% q-o-q to MYR1.3 trillion. At the end of 2023, DanaInfra Nasional, a finance company owned by the government, had the most outstanding LCY corporate bonds at MYR82.8 billion.

Figure 2: Composition of Local Currency Bonds Outstanding in Malaysia

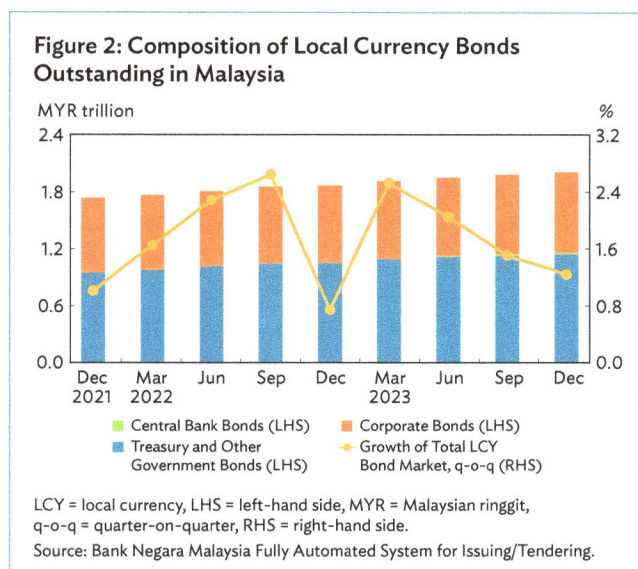

LCY = local currency, LHS = left-hand side, MYR = Malaysian ringgit, q-o-q = quarter-on-quarter, RHS = right-hand side.
Source: Bank Negara Malaysia Fully Automated System for Issuing/Tendering.

This market summary was written by Patrick Vincent Lubenia, consultant, Economic Research and Development Impact Department, ADB, Manila.

Issuance of LCY bonds in Malaysia declined during the review period due to reduced issuance of government securities. LCY bond sales dropped 12.2% q-o-q as fewer Treasury and other government bonds, and central bank bills, were issued during the quarter (**Figure 3**). The issuance of Malaysian Government Securities (conventional bonds) and Government Investment Issues, which are *sukuk* (Islamic bonds), likewise contracted in Q4 2023. LCY corporate bonds, on the other hand, increased 3.2% q-o-q. Cagamas, the mortgage corporation of Malaysia, continued to dominate all LCY corporate bond issuers in Q4 2023 with issuances totaling MYR8.1 billion.

Investor Profile

At the end of the third quarter of 2023, domestic investors held almost 80% of LCY government bonds outstanding (Figure 4). The largest holdings share belonged to financial institutions with 32.6% of total LCY government bonds. This was, however, lower than the 34.6% share they collectively held at the end of the third quarter of 2022. Increases in holdings shares were recorded for social security institutions, insurance companies, and Bank Negara Malaysia during the review period, while the share of foreign investors decreased.

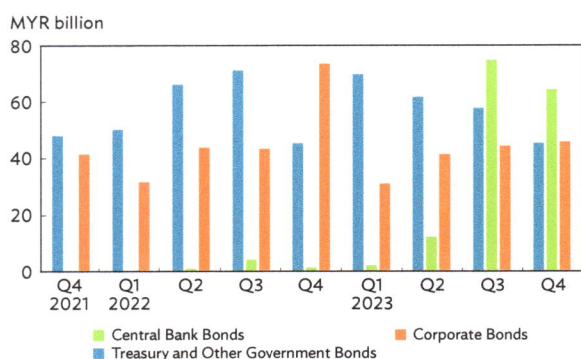

Figure 3: Composition of Local Currency Bond Issuance in Malaysia

MYR = Malaysian ringgit, Q1 = first quarter, Q2 = second quarter, Q3 = third quarter, Q4 = fourth quarter.
Source: Bank Negara Malaysia Fully Automated System for Issuing/Tendering.

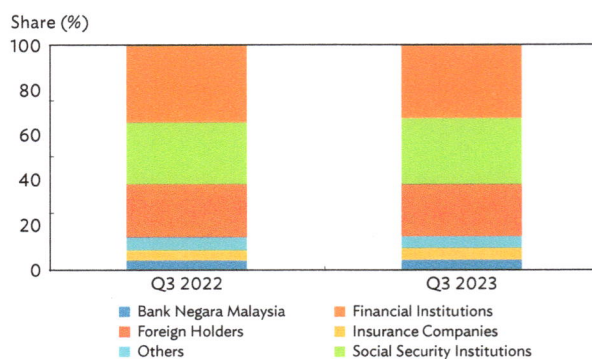

Figure 4: Local Currency Government Bonds Investor Profile

MYR = Malaysian ringgit, Q3 = third quarter.
Note: "Others" include statutory bodies, nominees and trustee companies, and cooperatives and unclassified items.
Source: Bank Negara Malaysia.

Philippines

Yield Movements

Local currency (LCY) government bond yields in the Philippines rose for nearly all tenors between 1 December 2023 and 29 February 2024 as the Bangko Sentral ng Pilipinas held its policy rate near a 17-year high (**Figure 1**). Despite improvements in domestic inflation conditions, the Bangko Sentral ng Pilipinas, in its 14 February policy meeting, kept its overnight reverse repurchase rate steady at 6.50% to firmly anchor inflation expectations within the target range amid risks brought about by elevated fuel prices and the "El Niño" climate phenomenon's impact on food prices. The increase in yields was also influenced by the government's retail bond offering during 13–23 February amid upward market adjustments based on the Retail Treasury Bond rate.

Local Currency Bond Market Size and Issuance

The Philippines' LCY bond market expanded 1.0% quarter-on-quarter (q-o-q) in the fourth quarter (Q4) of 2023, driven by growth in government bonds (**Figure 2**). Treasury and other government bonds outstanding, which accounted for 82.1% of the total LCY debt stock at the end of December, grew 2.1% q-o-q in Q4 2023, up from 0.3% q-o-q in the previous quarter. Despite a contraction in issuance, government bonds grew due to a low volume of maturities during the quarter. On the other hand, outstanding central bank securities contracted 6.2% q-o-q due to a large volume of maturities in Q4 2023 that exceeded total issuance. The LCY corporate bond stock contracted 2.6% q-o-q, falling to PHP1.5 trillion at the end of December, driven by a large number of bond maturities during the quarter. Corporate bonds accounted for 12.6% of the total LCY debt stock at the end of December, with the largest share coming from the property sector accounting for 31.6% of this total.

Figure 1: The Philippines' Benchmark Yield Curve— Local Currency Government Bonds

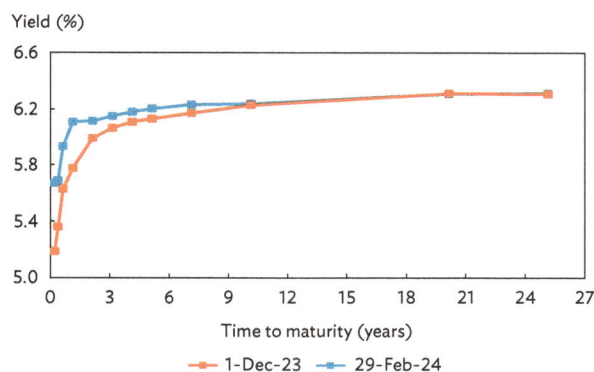

Source: Based on data from Bloomberg LP.

Figure 2: Composition of Local Currency Bonds Outstanding in the Philippines

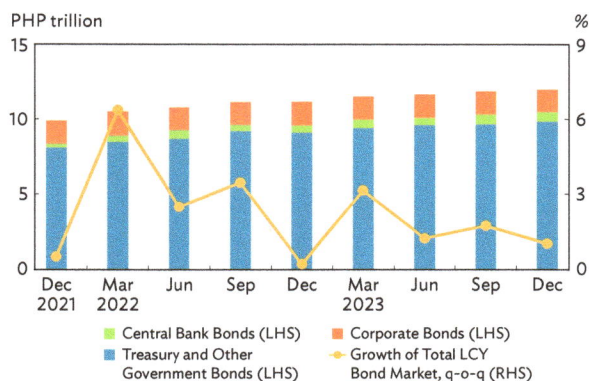

LCY = local currency, LHS = left-hand side, PHP = Philippine peso, q-o-q = quarter-on-quarter, RHS = right-hand side.

Note: Treasury and other government bonds comprise Treasury bonds, Treasury bills, and bonds issued by government agencies, entities, and corporations for which repayment is guaranteed by the Government of the Philippines. This includes bonds issued by Power Sector Assets and Liabilities Management and the National Food Authority, among others.

Sources: Bureau of the Treasury and Bloomberg LP.

This market summary was written by Jeremy Grace Ilustrisimo, consultant, Economic Research and Development Impact Department, ADB, Manila.

A decline in government bond issuance drove the market's LCY bond issuance to contract 4.4% q-o-q in Q4 2023 (Figure 3). Issuance of Treasury and other government bonds contracted 26.2% q-o-q in Q4 2023, as the government reduced borrowing by 73% to PHP60.0 billion in December amid a shrinking budget deficit that eased pressure on the government's debt financing. In addition, the Bureau of the Treasury met its domestic funding requirements for 2023 at its 5 December auction, resulting in the cancellation of the year's remaining auction scheduled on 11 December. Meanwhile, central bank securities issuance grew 0.9% q-o-q in Q4 2023 as the government mopped up excess liquidity in the economy to control inflation. Corporate bond issuance grew 85.5% q-o-q in Q4 2023 from a relatively low base in the previous quarter. However, total LCY corporate bond issuance in 2023 only reached PHP205.5 billion, which was 58.6% lower than in 2022 amid the uncertain environment triggered by the aggressive rate hikes of the Bangko Sentral ng Pilipinas beginning in May 2022. Consequently, only five firms tapped the bond market for funding during the quarter, with the largest issuance coming from the Bank of the Philippine Islands whose debt sales amounted to PHP36.6 billion.

Investor Profile

The investor landscape in the Philippines' LCY government bond market remained mostly unchanged in 2023 (Figure 4). The Philippines' LCY government bond market remains consistently dominated by two investor groups: (i) banks and investment houses, and (ii) contractual savings institutions and tax-exempt institutions. These two investor groups comprised a combined bond holdings equivalent to 78.1% of total LCY government bonds outstanding at the end of December 2023. Banks and investment houses remained the single-largest investor group, constituting 46.2% of total LCY bonds outstanding. Among all other investor groups, only banks and investment houses posted an increase (2.2%) in their bond holdings share in 2023. Contractual savings institutions and tax-exempt institutions remained the second-largest investor group, with their holdings share edging down to 31.9% in December 2023 from 33.5% in the prior year.

Figure 3: Composition of Local Currency Bond Issuance in the Philippines

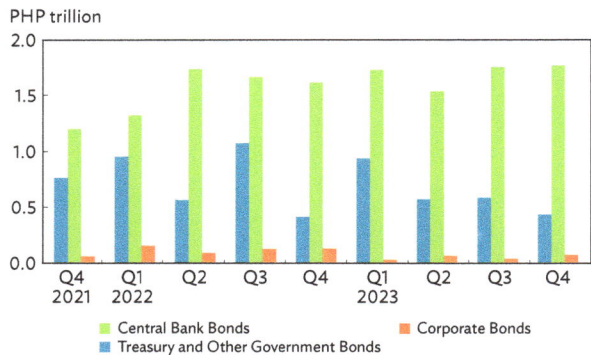

PHP = Philippine peso, Q1 = first quarter, Q2 = second quarter, Q3 = third quarter, Q4 = fourth quarter.

Note: Treasury and other government bonds comprise Treasury bonds, Treasury bills, and bonds issued by government agencies, entities, and corporations for which repayment is guaranteed by the Government of the Philippines. This includes bonds issued by Power Sector Assets and Liabilities Management and the National Food Authority, among others.

Sources: Bureau of the Treasury and Bloomberg LP.

Figure 4: Investor Profile of Local Currency Government Bonds

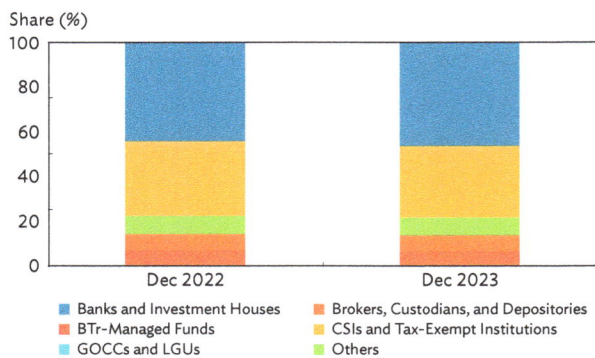

BTr = Bureau of the Treasury, CSI = contractual savings institution, GOCC = government-owned or -controlled corporation, LGU = local government unit.

Note: At the end of December 2023, government-owned or -controlled corporations and local government units' holdings share was 0.02%, amounting to PHP2.4 billion.

Source: Bureau of the Treasury.

Singapore

Yield Movements

Between 1 December 2023 and 29 February 2024, movements in Singapore's local currency (LCY) government bond yields were mixed (Figure 1). The mixed movement was due to uncertainties in the timing of monetary policy easing by the United States Federal Reserve. Yields from 2 years to 20 years increased an average of 6 basis points, while yields at both ends of the curve declined an average of 14 basis points. The uptick in the yields of intermediate tenors tracked the movement in yields of United States Treasuries, which generally rose during the review period. The Monetary Authority of Singapore left its monetary policy stance unchanged at its 29 January meeting, maintaining the rate of appreciation of the Singapore dollar nominal effective exchange rate.

Local Currency Bond Market Size and Issuance

By the end of Q4 2023, growth in the LCY bond market of Singapore was led by an increase in government bonds outstanding. LCY bonds outstanding jumped 2.6% quarter-on-quarter (q-o-q) to reach SGD715.6 billion (**Figure 2**). This expansion was due to the increase in outstanding Treasury and other government securities, and central bank securities, which climbed 2.9% q-o-q and 5.3% q-o-q, respectively. On the other hand, outstanding LCY corporate bonds declined 2.3% q-o-q by the end of December. The government-owned Housing & Development Board continued to have the most LCY corporate bonds outstanding by the end of 2023 at SGD27.1 billion.

Figure 1: Singapore's Benchmark Yield Curve—Local Currency Government Bonds

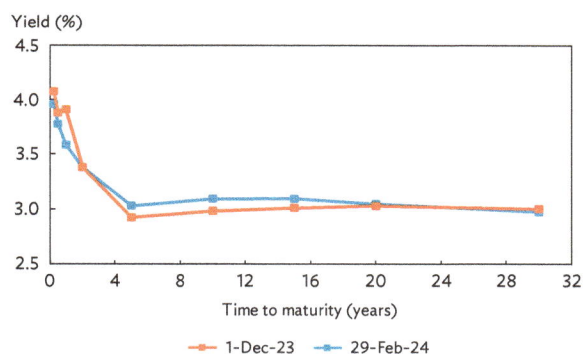

Source: Based on data from Bloomberg LP.

Figure 2: Composition of Local Currency Bonds Outstanding in Singapore

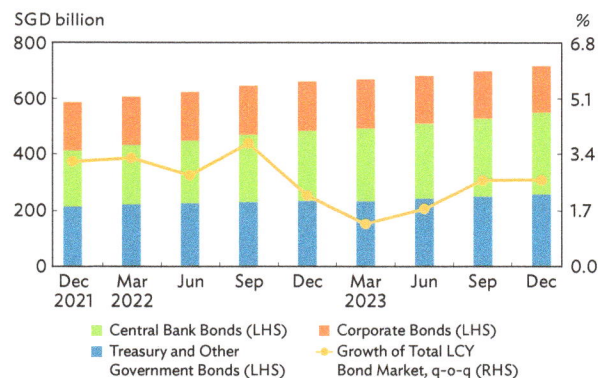

LCY = local currency, LHS = left-hand side, q-o-q = quarter-on-quarter, RHS = right-hand side, SGD = Singapore dollar.
Note: Corporate bonds are based on *AsianBondsOnline* estimates.
Sources: Monetary Authority of Singapore and Bloomberg LP.

This market summary was written by Patrick Vincent Lubenia, consultant, Economic Research and Development Impact Department, ADB, Manila.

In Q4 2023, growth in the issuance of LCY bonds decelerated from the previous quarter as Treasury issuance dropped. LCY bond issuance in Q4 2023 increased 4.9% q-o-q, driven by growth in central bank bills and corporate bonds. However, this was offset by a decline in issuance of Treasury and other government bonds, which fell 5.0% q-o-q (**Figure 3**). Corporate bond issuance reached SGD1.9 billion during the quarter on growth of 46.2% q-o-q. The Housing & Development Board had the single-largest issuance during the quarter with a SGD740.0 million 5-year bond issued in November.

Figure 3: Composition of Local Currency Bond Issuance in Singapore

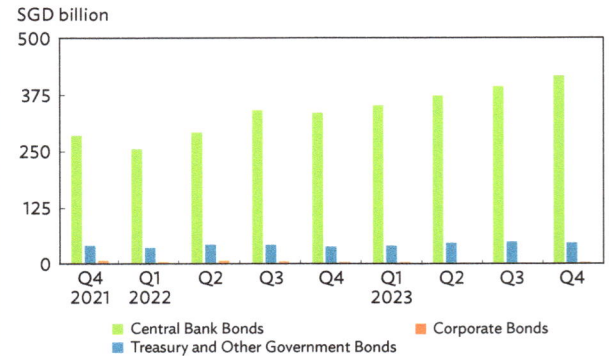

Q1 = first quarter, Q2 = second quarter, Q3 = third quarter, Q4 = fourth quarter, SGD = Singapore dollar.

Note: Corporate bonds are based on *AsianBondsOnline* estimates.

Sources: Monetary Authority of Singapore and Bloomberg LP.

Thailand

Yield Movements

Between 1 December 2023 and 29 February 2024, Thailand's local currency (LCY) government bond yields fell for all tenors except short-term bonds (Figure 1). The decline in yields for most bonds followed the regional trend of falling bond yields amid moderating inflation and market expectations that the United States Federal Reserve would start cutting interest rates in the second half of 2024. Meanwhile, short-term bond yields in Thailand increased as interest rates remained elevated in the near term, with the Bank of Thailand (BOT) holding its policy rate unchanged at a record high of 2.50% during its 7 February meeting. Weak inflation also contributed to the decline in bond yields. Thailand's headline inflation was –0.8% year-on-year in February, marking the fourth consecutive month of deflation.

Local Currency Bond Market Size and Issuance

Thailand's LCY bond market contracted 0.5% quarter-on-quarter (q-o-q) in the fourth quarter (Q4) of 2023, totaling THB16.5 trillion at the end of December (Figure 2). Due to weak issuance and a high volume of maturities, outstanding BOT bonds contracted 8.9% q-o-q in Q4 2023, outweighing tepid growth in outstanding Treasury and other government bonds (1.0% q-o-q) and corporate bonds (1.1% q-o-q). At the end of December, Treasury and other government bonds (THB9.4 trillion) comprised 57.1% of Thailand's LCY bond market. Corporate bonds (THB4.8 trillion) and BOT bonds (THB2.2 trillion) accounted for the remaining shares of 29.4% and 13.5%, respectively.

Figure 1: Thailand's Benchmark Yield Curve— Local Currency Government Bonds

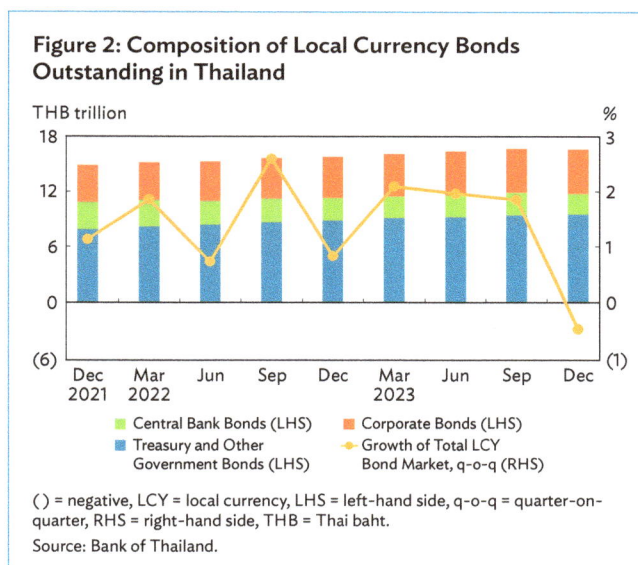

Sources: Based on data from Bloomberg LP and Thai Bond Market Association.

Figure 2: Composition of Local Currency Bonds Outstanding in Thailand

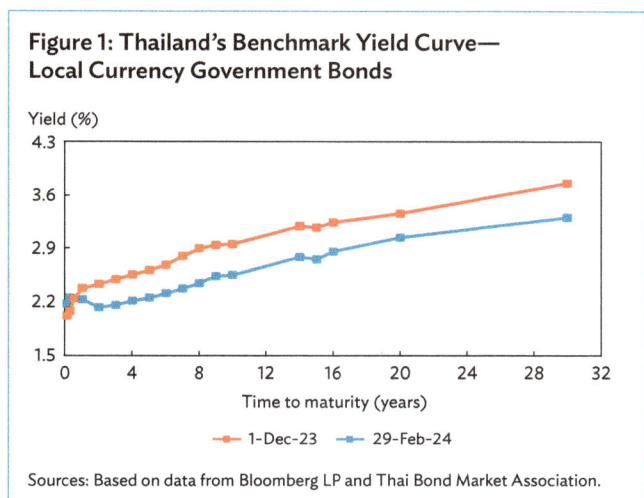

( ) = negative, LCY = local currency, LHS = left-hand side, q-o-q = quarter-on-quarter, RHS = right-hand side, THB = Thai baht.
Source: Bank of Thailand.

This market summary was written by Debbie Gundaya, consultant, Economic Research and Development Impact Department, ADB, Manila.

LCY bond issuance fell 11.3% q-o-q to THB2.0 trillion in Q4 2023 as bond sales contracted for all bond market segments. Treasury and other government bond issuance declined 8.9% q-o-q to THB488.3 billion in Q4 2023, partly due to the delayed approval of the fiscal year 2024 budget (**Figure 3**). Meanwhile, BOT bond issuance totaled THB1.0 trillion in Q4 2023, down 14.3% q-o-q. Corporate debt issuance also fell 6.7% q-o-q to THB457.8 billion in Q4 2023 amid elevated borrowing rates. BTS Group was the top issuer in Q4 2023, with a total of THB15.1 billion in new issuance.

Figure 3: Composition of Local Currency Bond Issuance in Thailand

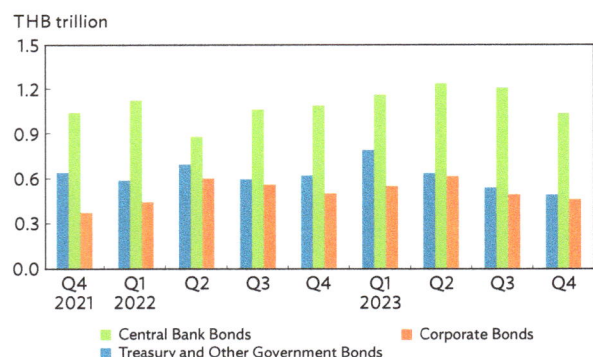

THB trillion

Q1 = first quarter, Q2 = second quarter, Q3 = third quarter, Q4 = fourth quarter, THB = Thai baht.
Source: Bank of Thailand.

Investor Profile

Domestic investors still dominate the Thai LCY government bond market. The share of Thai LCY government bonds held by domestic investors rose to 89.3% at the end of December 2023 from 87.2% a year earlier, driven primarily by increased holdings among banks, and insurance and pension funds (**Figure 4**). In contrast, foreign holders' share decreased to 10.7% from 12.8% during the same period, largely due to relatively higher returns in developed markets like the United States as global rates remained elevated. Meanwhile, the BOT's holdings of LCY government bonds increased from 5.8% to 6.5% from December 2022 to December 2023, as the central bank purchased a total of THB76.5 billion of government bonds in 2023 to help stabilize the LCY bond market. Among investor groups, insurance and pension funds held the largest share of LCY government bonds at 44.5% at the end of December 2023.

Figure 4: Investor Profile of Government Bonds in Thailand

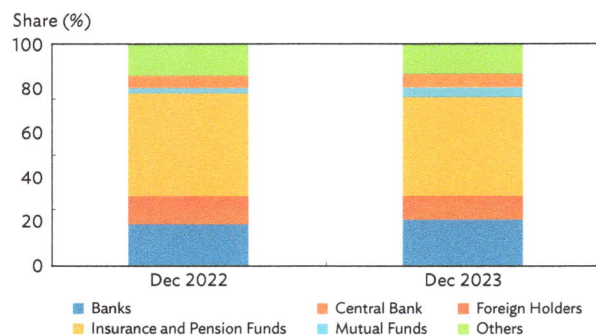

Share (%)

Source: Bank of Thailand.

Viet Nam

Yield Movements

Local currency (LCY) government bond yields in Viet Nam declined for most tenors between 1 December 2023 and 29 February 2024 amid uncertainties in the timing of policy rate cuts by the United States Federal Reserve (**Figure 1**). The decline in yields was also driven by the central bank holding rates steady since July 2023 to help prop up economic growth. In 2023, the central bank reduced its refinancing rate by a cumulative total of 150 basis points from April to June 2023. Per a news release from *Vietnamnet Global*, the State Bank of Vietnam (SBV), early this year, expressed its intention to not increase the policy rate in 2024 to support economic growth. Viet Nam's economy grew 5.1% year-on-year in 2023, lower than the government's target growth of 6.5%.

Local Currency Bond Market Size and Issuance

Viet Nam's LCY bond market contracted 0.4% quarter-on-quarter (q-o-q) in the fourth quarter (Q4) of 2023 due to a large volume of maturities of central bank securities (**Figure 2**). In Q4 2023, a total of VND360.3 trillion of central bank securities matured, while the SBV ceased issuing securities on 9 November. The central bank decided to halt its securities issuance—as overnight interbank interest rates climbed amid adjustments to the banking system's short-term liquidity—providing indirect support to the foreign exchange rate. Growth in outstanding government bonds moderated to 2.0% q-o-q from 2.6% q-o-q growth in the third quarter of 2023 on reduced issuance. Corporate bonds outstanding rebounded in Q4 2023, posting an increase of 6.8% q-o-q compared with a decline of 2.9% q-o-q in the previous quarter, as issuers returned amid improved investor sentiment following reforms in the corporate bond market.

Figure 1: Viet Nam's Benchmark Yield Curve—Local Currency Government Bonds

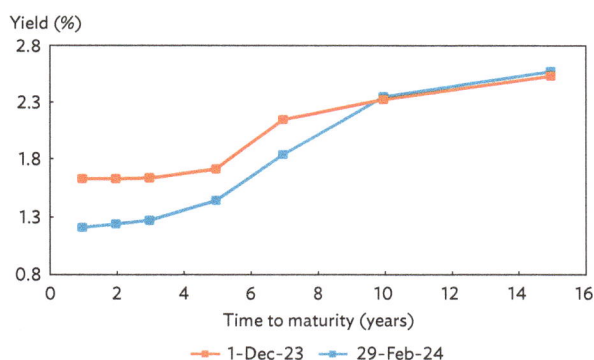

Source: Based on data from Bloomberg LP.

Figure 2: Composition of Local Currency Bonds Outstanding in Viet Nam

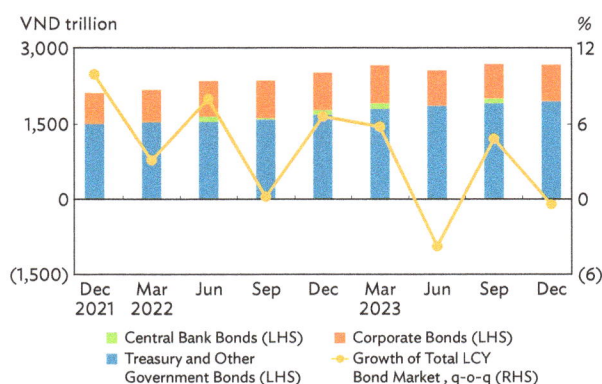

( ) = negative, LCY = local currency, LHS = left-hand side, q-o-q = quarter-on-quarter, RHS = right-hand side, VND = Vietnamese dong.
Note: Other government bonds comprise government-guaranteed and municipal bonds.
Sources: Vietnam Bond Market Association and Bloomberg LP.

This market summary was written by Jeremy Grace Ilustrisimo, consultant, Economic Research and Development Impact Department, ADB, Manila.

Total LCY bond issuance grew 81.6% q-o-q in Q4 2023 on increased issuance from corporates and the central bank (Figure 3). Corporate bond issuance expanded 72.1% q-o-q in Q4 2023 to reach VND92.6 trillion amid a gradual recovery in Viet Nam's corporate bond market. The government's implementation of strict regulations for the issuance of corporate bonds, combined with banks' low deposit interest rates, provided support for corporate bond issuance. The banking sector remained the largest issuer of corporate bonds in Viet Nam, accounting for 64.6% of all LCY corporate bonds issued in Q4 2023, with Orient Commercial Joint Stock Bank as the top issuer during the quarter on aggregated debt sales of VND9.3 trillion. To adjust short-term liquidity in the banking system, which is expected to lift the LCY-denominated interest rates in the interbank market and support the Vietnamese dong, the SBV's securities issuance in October increased to VND225.3 trillion, more than double the issuance volume of VND93.8 trillion in September. On the other hand, issuance of government bonds contracted 43.5% q-o-q as the State Treasury of Vietnam reduced issuance in Q4 2023 while closely monitoring market movements to ensure the government's debt servicing.

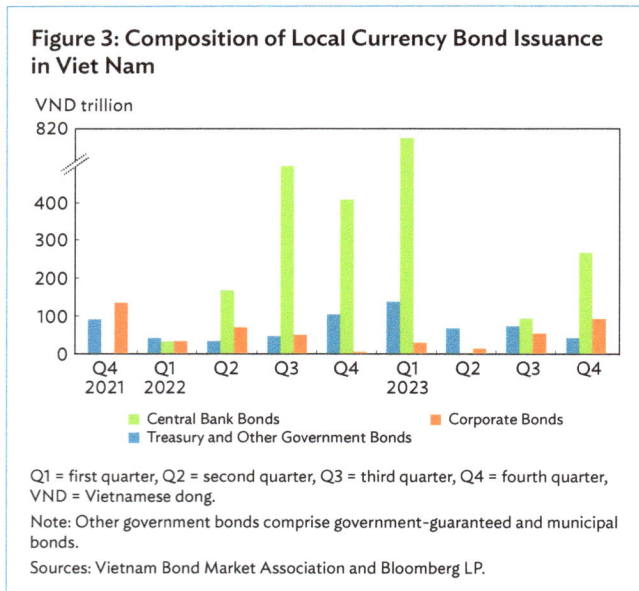

Investor Profile

A majority of Viet Nam's LCY government bonds outstanding were held by insurance firms and banks at the end of December 2023 (Figure 4). Similar to December 2022, the collective holdings shares of insurance firms and banks accounted for 99.4% of the LCY government bond market. Insurance companies remained the single-largest investor group, with their holdings share inching up to 59.7% at the end of December 2023 from 58.9% a year earlier. On the other hand, banks' holdings share edged down to 39.6% from 40.5% in the same period. Due to having only two dominant investor groups in its LCY government bond market, Viet Nam continued to have the highest Herfindahl–Hirschman Index score among its regional peers at the end of December 2023.[12]

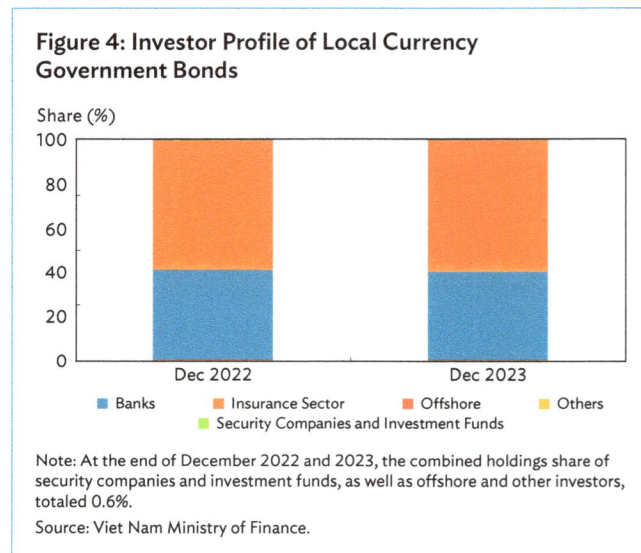

Figure 3: Composition of Local Currency Bond Issuance in Viet Nam

Q1 = first quarter, Q2 = second quarter, Q3 = third quarter, Q4 = fourth quarter, VND = Vietnamese dong.

Note: Other government bonds comprise government-guaranteed and municipal bonds.

Sources: Vietnam Bond Market Association and Bloomberg LP.

Figure 4: Investor Profile of Local Currency Government Bonds

Note: At the end of December 2022 and 2023, the combined holdings share of security companies and investment funds, as well as offshore and other investors, totaled 0.6%.

Source: Viet Nam Ministry of Finance.

---

12   The Herfindahl–Hirschman Index is a commonly accepted measure of market concentration. The index is used to measure the investor profile diversification of the local currency bond market and is calculated by summing the squared share of each investor group in the bond market.